CANARIES IN COLOUR

CANARIES
IN COLOUR

by
GEORGE LYNCH

Illustrated by
M. McGREGOR

BLANDFORD PRESS

POOLE   DORSET

First published in 1971
Reprinted 1976
Reprinted 1979
Copyright © 1971 Blandford Press Ltd
Link House, West Street
Poole, Dorset BH15 1LL

ISBN 0 7137 0540 X

Coloured illustrations reproduced and printed by
Colour Reproduction Ltd., Billericay, Essex

Set in Photon Times 10 pt. by
Richard Clay (The Chaucer Press), Ltd., Bungay, Suffolk
and printed in Great Britain by
Fletcher & Son Ltd, Norwich

CONTENTS

LIST OF ILLUSTRATIONS

PREFACE

This book has been written for those who breed canaries and for the thousands of people who keep a single bird at home. Both kinds of canary-lover will, I hope, find this book full of valuable information and even the experienced breeder should find some helpful hints and tips. I have dealt with all the known varieties found in Britain, and given details of show cages, scales of points, etc., in the section on the Exhibition Canary, while at the same time giving special mention to those canaries that are suitable as pets to be kept in the home.

George Lynch
*President, the National
Council of Aviculture,
and President, the Old
Varieties Canary Association*

PART ONE

KEEPING CANARIES

1. A SHORT HISTORY OF THE CANARY

All the different types of canary that we know today are descended from the wild canary (*Serinus canarius*). The first reference to this bird is in Gesner's *Historia Animalium* (1555) where he refers to 'a bird of sweetest song brought from the Canary Islands' which was $4\frac{1}{2}$–5 inches (11–12 cm.) in length. As can be seen from plate 1, it is quite nondescript in appearance, and comparison with modern canaries shows how much the breeders have accomplished over the years.

In 1478 the Canary Islands were conquered by the Spaniards and wild canaries were brought back to Spain in large numbers. The singing canary became very popular, and wealthy Spaniards paid high prices for these highly desirable ladies' pets. A lucrative trade was developed, and canaries were exported all over Europe. The Spaniards were careful to sell only the male birds, and thus retained a monopoly for nearly a hundred years; but in the middle of the sixteenth century, as we know from Giovanni Pietro Olina's *Ucceliera*, published in Rome in 1622, all this came to an end. A Spanish vessel, bound for Leghorn and carrying a large number of canaries, was wrecked; many of the birds escaped or were freed and were blown by the prevailing winds to the island of Elba, where they found living conditions ideal and began to breed and multiply considerably. Before long they were discovered there by the Italians, who not only sold them but started to breed them in quantity on the Italian mainland and to export them, firstly to all the countries of central Europe and eventually to the rest of Europe, including Russia and England. In the middle of the seventeenth century the Germans also were exporting canaries, called 'German birds', which later developed into the Roller canary.

About 1713 Hervieux listed 20 varieties of canary and some other birds, but these were not distinct breeds so much as colour variations. Included among these varieties were the Lizard and the London Fancy, also Cinnamons, Crests and Whites. The Crest is often mentioned, but it is most likely that the birds were quite different then; thus the London Fancy is described as yellow with jet-black spots, whereas we know it as a yellow bird with jet-black wings and tail.

Canary-fancying actually started in the eighteenth century. Up till then wealthy people had kept the birds in large aviaries for the beauty of their song; now working people had them in small cages and the Fancy was born. Over all these years the canary has maintained its popularity, and today, despite competition from the budgerigar, more canaries are bred than ever before. Although the budgerigar has become the Number One pet bird, canaries easily outnumber budgerigars at most mixed shows in Britain.

2. BUYING STOCK FOR BREEDING

My advice to the beginner is to make a start with one of the smaller varieties such as the Gloster, Border or Lizard (see pp. 101, 103, 109). These are all free breeders and, what may be more important, are reasonably priced and easily obtained. Should you have a strong preference for one of the other breeds, however, by all means carry on with that variety, especially if you have someone to advise you.

Many people starting in the hobby buy good birds from several leading breeders and consequently pay big prices for them. For a couple of seasons they win red tickets, cups, etc., showing in the novice classes, and they soon become champions, but then they find they have to dig deeply into their pockets for more winners as they have failed to breed them. It is only a matter of time before they go out of the Fancy altogether.

October or November is the best month for buying stock, since this gives the birds plenty of time to settle down in their new breeding quarters. For those buying pets, however, any time will do, except for July and August, which is the moulting period.

Remember that winners do not necessarily breed winners. If, for instance, it were possible to buy the best yellow cock of your breed at the National Show and the best buff hen, bred by two different breeders, it is quite likely that they would not produce good birds when mated. I strongly advise intending breeders to join their local Cage Bird Society, to go to one of its leading breeders of the chosen variety and to say: 'I am interested in your breed of birds. I would like to place myself in your hands, I can afford so much, and I am prepared to wait until you can fix me up.' By this means you can obtain in one year a stud of birds that has taken the breeder many years and a great deal of money to establish. They will all be line-bred, and you can breed youngsters from them to beat those of the original breeder the following year! This is no pipe-dream: it occurs again and again. Furthermore, most breeders will take an interest in you and what is after all their own stud of birds thereafter. Under these circumstances, never be tempted to introduce other birds into the stud, however good they may seem to be. Should you require a particular bird or birds, go back to the original breeder. There will come a time when you want an outcross, but that will not be for several years, and by then you will have gained some experience.

If for any reason you cannot follow this advice and have to buy where you can, there is one golden rule: on no account buy flighted hens. Only unflighted hens should be considered. If a breeder has a young hen that lays a full clutch of eggs, sits, hatches and rears without trouble, she is worth her weight in diamonds, and he is not going to part with her, but the hens that let him down—the non- or two-egg layers; those that refuse to feed the young; those that pluck the young when the feathers first appear—these he will be anxious to dispose of and they are the birds you do *not* want. Over-year cocks are quite satisfactory to buy; in fact, for breeding purposes I prefer these to unflighted birds.

I know good fanciers who have been breeding canaries for over 40 years without ever achieving more than an occasional red ticket in small classes. The main reason is that they have not got a stud of birds, just a collection. I cannot emphasise too strongly that if you want to succeed in this highly competitive fancy you must line-breed. Remember that like, when bred to like, will produce like. Over the years I have found that a good stud of canaries will produce about 70 per cent young of equal standard to their own; about 20 per cent slightly inferior; 5 per cent very poor (you wonder how on earth these birds turned up); and 5 per cent a little better, perhaps a 'stormer' here. These last birds are going to maintain and improve the stud, and on no account should they be sold even if the offer made is very tempting.

The pet bird should be purchased from a canary breeder or a good pet shop. It is essential to buy a young healthy cock bird. The hens do not sing, and the cocks will sing if in good health from November until July when they undergo the annual moult. Never buy a bird that is soiled around the vent, or one whose tail is gently moving up and down in a pumping manner. If possible, it is always wise to take an experienced breeder with you when buying, but if you hear a bird singing, then you can regard it as an infallible sign that it is in good health. The following canaries make excellent pets as they are reasonable in price and easy to look after: the Gloster canary, sometimes known as the Beatle bird as it has a little crest of feathers on its head which reminds people of the hairstyle of this famous pop group; the Border canary and the Fife Fancy. There is, of course, the Roller which will give pleasure to many with its continuous low, sweet notes, but to make sure of this song you will have to get a trained bird, since many so-called Rollers are just 'mongrels' that will sing like an ordinary canary. All these birds are dealt with later in the book.

3. LIVING QUARTERS

Canaries can be—and indeed have been—bred in all kinds of places, such as old sheds, aviaries, workshops, bedrooms, prisons and specially designed birdrooms. They are most adaptable birds, and provided they are sufficiently healthy will try to produce young under the most unlikely conditions and in seemingly unsuitable accommodation. If they are to be kept purely for pleasure, then an outdoor aviary with a good shelter is ideal, but if breeding for show is the aim, then a good birdroom is essential. A room in the house is excellent as long as it does not face north, or a good shed can often be converted into a birdroom by the addition of a large window, ventilation and so on.

There are some rules that should be followed in all birdrooms. Although good ventilation is vital and you cannot have too much fresh air, it is essential that there are no draughts as these can be fatal to all birds. Plenty of daylight is also necessary, but make sure that this does not cause fluctuations in temperature. Last but not least, ensure that the room is free from furry pests; mice in particular will find a way in if at all possible. One good plan for circumventing pests is to raise the birdroom about 2 feet from the ground on concrete pillars. On top of each pillar fix one of the old-fashioned metal electric light shades which look like a mandarin's hat; no vermin will be able to pass these and get into the birdroom. I cannot stress too strongly the importance of a mouse-free birdroom.

One of the main objections to a concrete floor in a birdroom used to be that damp seeped through and made the floor cold. Today, builders lay a sheet of polythene on the ground before spreading the concrete; this keeps the damp out, and tiles can safely be laid directly on the concrete.

It is important to decide how many pairs you intend to breed from. For those who are away at work all day I consider 12 pairs the absolute maximum, and would advise no more than eight. For 12 breeding pairs, a room of 14 × 8 feet (4·2 × 2·4 metres) is necessary, preferably facing south-east or east; in this position the birds will gain all the advantages of the early sun, which is most important when rearing is taking place, and will not be exposed to the high temperatures of a summer afternoon. (As already stated, facing north is to be avoided.)

4. HEATING AND LIGHTING

If all artificial heating and lighting were eliminated, many more birds would be bred each year. Too much artificial light brings on soft moult (see p. 22), and too much heat weakens the birds when they go to shows and may bring them on into breeding condition too early. I use neither artificial light nor heat in my birdroom, but realise that some light is essential when owners have to go out to work, for in the winter-time it is dark when they leave and return. Nevertheless, artificial light should be kept to the absolute minimum, and in the evenings the canaries should be attended to before anything else. Where it is essential to use light, a dimming device should be incorporated so that the birds have plenty of time to return to their favourite perch after they have been fed. In the United States, aviculturists have experimented with the use of light, and by slowly increasing it to about 20 hours a day have succeeded in getting canaries to nest and lay eggs by the end of December and beginning of January. There is no doubt, however, that the stamina of the birds is weakened under these conditions, and in any case there are no natural foods such as dandelion, chickweed, etc., available at that time of year.

Although I do not use heat myself, I cannot disagree with those who want a little warmth in the birdroom for their own comfort, or who say it is a great help during the early days of the breeding season; but I would emphasise that there should only be just enough heating to prevent the room temperature from falling below freezing point. The temperature should be thermostatically controlled, and the setting should not exceed $4 \cdot 5°C$ ($40°F$) except when birds are sitting or laying when a further $-15°C$ ($5°F$) could be added. If electricity is not available, then it is best not to use any heat at all. Oil stoves can be deadly and are not worth the risk.

5. FEEDING

It is obvious that feeding time is the most important even in the life of a canary, and that the finest birdroom in the world is wasted if the stock is fed incorrectly. I could now start blinding the reader with science, talking about carbohydrates, proteins, fats, oils and trace elements, and produce elaborate charts analysing the food value of different seeds. I do not intend to do this. Our forefathers successfully bred canaries without any knowledge of these matters; indeed, one can be badly misled by such information even today, because modern methods of growing, harvesting and ripening can produce seed with virtually no food value, and this occurs with canary seed (the birds' main diet) which I will refer to later.

If you have only one or two pet birds, then I strongly recommend the packet seeds from one of the well-known pet food suppliers. These are clean, balanced and usually include seeds prepared to supply all necessary vitamins. The breeder, however, must buy in bulk—it would be far too costly to buy dozens of packets of seed for his stud. For many years the basic diet used by most breeders in their seed-hoppers has been a mixture of plain canary and red rape seed, in a proportion of two or three parts of canary to one of rape; in addition, twice or three times a week they feed a small amount of mixed seed, including hemp, teazle, niger, black rape, linseed and oats. Every now and again a spoonful of condition seed is added—this includes gold of pleasure as well as some of those already mentioned—lettuce, dandelion, maw and a number of wild seeds. When the breeding season is approaching, a little niger seed should be given to the hens about three times a week; this is an oily seed and is said to prevent egg-binding (see p. 33).

It cannot be too strongly stressed that 'ringing the changes' is much appreciated by the stock and helps to keep them fit and well. Some years ago I had a very bad breeding season and all the birds seemed to be below par. I used then to buy two hundredweight of canary seed which lasted all the year; following a tip from a friend I had this analysed and found that its feeding value was practically nil—my birds were in fact half-starved. Since then I have played safe and bought a hundredweight of mixed plain canary seed at a time. This contains seed from Australia, Morocco, Spain and other countries, and one knows that even if one country of origin has a bad ripening year it is unlikely that all will suffer in this way. I now use the following as my basic diet: six parts of canary seed, one part red rape, one part black rape, one part niger and half a part of linseed. These are all thoroughly mixed together and used in the hoppers. I only use hemp seed and teazle when they have been thoroughly soaked; two parts of teazle and one of hemp should be placed in water and left for 48 hours, then turned into the strainer and washed under the tap in running water. This is given twice weekly, but is used daily when young are in the nest; I also feed it to the young when first weaned. From the supplier of the canary seed I also obtain an excellent conditioning seed called 'tonic grains'. This contains all the conditioning seeds I have already mentioned plus a great many more, and I give the birds about a teaspoonful each twice a week. The basic diet I now use was suggested to me by Mr P. W. Butler, and this is a good opportunity to pay him my tribute. He has been a good friend of mine for over 40 years, and in my opinion is one of the 'great' canary breeders—a really dedicated fancier. The special perch, the cuttlefish holder, special seedhopper and a number of other feeding and rearing hints have come from him over the years.

Greenstuff is very important to canaries; it has not a great deal of food value, but is rich in both minerals and vitamins. Practically any kind of green food is acceptable, certainly any of the *Brassica* family that we grow in our gardens or can purchase in the shops. During the winter the birds should be given some of this twice a week; not a lot—a single sprout leaf per bird is sufficient, and perhaps a piece of sweet apple. But when spring is approaching I forget all these, and directly dandelion is available I feed this daily. The whole plant should be dug up, complete with the root, as the birds love to eat it all. Later on when the plant flowers, I wait until the white fluff shows, then pick the stalk and, by holding the seeding head in one hand and twisting the fluff off with the other, obtain a green cup full of seed. Some of the seed will be unripe, but all the birds love it and it acts as a first-class tonic. The main reason for removing the fluff is that it goes on growing and would, if left, fill the cages with fluffy down.

Later on in spring, seeding chickweed can be given, and in my opinion this is the greatest food of all; it can be used *ad lib* without worry or trouble. (In this connection there is an amusing story about Mr Butler, when he gave a talk on canary breeding at a well-known Cage Bird Society in Bucks. He waxed eloquent about chickweed, saying that he gathered this by the sackful and spread it all over the floor, right up to the birds' knees. Later in the year he judged this

Club's Young Stock Show and, after he had finished, a novice thanked him for his advice about the chickweed; he said that this was by far the best breeding season he had ever known, since he had bred over 60 Border canaries and had won most of the classes at that day's Show. The Secretary confirmed this, and at the request of the novice both men agreed to go and inspect the birds at his home a short distance away. When they arrived at the birdroom the young man pushed and heaved and eventually managed to force the door open; there on the birdroom floor was chickweed right up to the knees of the visitors—but not a trace in the cages! The young man had of course misunderstood Mr Butler, but he had still had a wonderful season; perhaps this was due to the extra humidity caused by all this greenstuff, who knows?)

Suitable soft food usually takes the form of egg mixed with biscuit meal, or one of the excellent proprietary soft foods sold in packet form. Many of the latter are a complete food in themselves, but even so I think it best to add a hard-boiled egg that has been sieved or grated, especially if the food is being used for rearing purposes. This soft food can be given about once a week during the winter, increasing to three or four times weekly as the breeding season approaches. Bread and milk, or milk sop, is very good and is one of the best sources of the amino-acids which are so essential for good feather growth. Grit is also essential; buy mixed grit which includes sand, shell and flintstone, plus other mineral supplements. I live near the sea and so I use fine sea grit, to which I add crushed oyster shell; I have found this very good over the years.

Now for a few words of warning. Be very careful about where you gather your green food, including chickweed. Due to the insecticides and weedkillers used in great quantities nowadays, very many birds have been poisoned, and some of the sprays can drift on the wind for great distances. A few years ago I collected some chickweed from a piece of ground that had lain fallow for over a year; since the ground was nearly surrounded by sea I knew it was safe from any insecticide spray drift. It was towards the end of May, and after liberally scattering this chickweed about the breeding cages I spent a day at the Chelsea Flower Show. When I returned, all the youngsters in the nest were dead, and the parents were not looking at all well. Suspecting the chickweed, I sent some away for analysis, and the report came back that the weed was loaded with arsenic. I later discovered that the farmer had used an arsenical type of weedkiller on a crop of wheat he had grown the previous year, and this had stayed in the ground and entered the chickweed. The quantity was not sufficient to kill an adult canary, but quite enough to kill the youngsters in the nest. Since then I have used only green food from my own garden, which covers half an acre. The fancier and the pet-bird owner must also be very careful in using lettuce during the winter months, since most of it comes from Holland where the growers use a fungicide to prevent base rot and this acts as a slow poison to the birds.

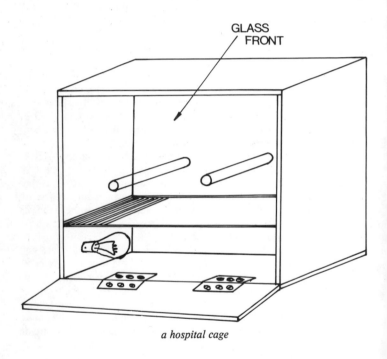

GLASS FRONT

a hospital cage

6. DISEASES AND ILLNESS

Birds can suffer from nearly as many diseases as humans. The diseases can be roughly classified under three main headings: Bacterial, Viruses and Fungus. Bacterial diseases include colds, which can vary considerably in severity. In some cases the feathers will be ruffled up, while the bird appears to be listless and stops feeding. In other cases the cold may develop into a serious complaint by travelling down the throat into the bronchi, where it causes pulmonary trouble. The usual cause of colds is a draught, and the cure is to keep the bird in a snug place, a hospital cage if you have one (see p. 20). If pulmonary trouble develops, place two or three drops of tincture of iodine in the drinking water until there is an improvement.

Avian tuberculosis is caused by the tubercle bacillus and is very infectious. The birds become listless, their droppings become very loose and they soon 'go light'. Death is only a matter of time.

Paratyphoid is found in all kinds of birds. It has been responsible for wiping out whole stocks of birds in private collections, birdrooms and pet shops. The main symptoms are displayed by the droppings, which become greenish and very loose. This disease does not kill all the birds, but survivors can pass the infection to any other birds with which they come into contact. It is best to clean everything out, disinfect very thoroughly and make a fresh start. While on this subject, it is very good management, before introducing any new bird into your room, to isolate it for a week to see if it remains 100 per cent active.

I suppose the best known of the Virus diseases is **Psittacosis** or parrot disease, which was responsible for the banning of all parrot-like birds from Britain for so many years, until it was discovered that nearly all species suffer from it. It is called Ornithosis when it occurs in all non-parrot-like birds. Both Psittacosis and Ornithosis can be caught by humans from birds. The symptoms are that the bird loses its vitality, sits on the perch looking very sorry for itself with closed eyes and refuses to eat; the droppings become very loose. Affected birds should be isolated and given a course of one of the antibiotics. I prefer Aureomycin myself.

Bronchitis is a virus disease which, contrary to general belief, is very infectious. When it strikes a bird many breeders think the trouble is caused by a cold. Affected birds may cough and have difficulty in breathing with the mouth wide open; they should be isolated at once and given the Aureomycin treatment. Should a bird have a discharge from the eyes and nostrils and appear to be in an advanced stage of bronchitis, it is best to have it destroyed.

The symptoms of **Newcastle disease** are very similar to those of bronchitis, but it can affect all kinds of birds and also human beings. A friend of mine had all his birds wiped out through the virus being brought into his room from a poultry farm next door. Twisting of the head and partial paralysis of the legs occur, and some birds are unable to eat. It is very contagious and the same treatment is advised as for bronchitis.

One trouble that the canary fancier is likely to encounter is **soft moult**, when some of the feathers keep on falling out during the non-moulting season. This is caused by one or more of the following: the bird is either in some kind of draught, or suffering from fluctuations of temperature, or is exposed to too much artificial light. The most usual cause with a fancier is too much artificial light. Owners of pet birds, however, are more likely to incur the disease as a result of fluctuating temperature, since they tend to keep the cage near a window which is the worst possible place. I use neither artificial heat nor light, and have not had a case of soft moult for many years, but it is quite common in the Fancy.

Slip claw is another problem which can ruin an exhibition bird; the hind claw of a bird suffering from this disease bends backwards, so that its foot cannot grip the perch but slips forward right off it. Opinions vary regarding the cause of this trouble, but I am convinced that it usually results from allowing the bird too much room when only about 5 weeks old, and also from giving it perches that are too hard and too large. The young bird then gets a sudden fright or is startled by some very minor incident and flies hard against the perch, knocking back the hind claw in which the tendons, etc., have not yet set. By using perching such as I shall describe (see pp. 27 and 28) this trouble should be avoided. The cure for slip claw is to use very thin perches, half the circumference of a lead pencil, or else perches can be dispensed with entirely and an inch or so of sawdust placed on the floor. I have cured this trouble by both methods, but prefer the thin perching—which should not be higher than 3 inches from the cage floor. Another possible problem is that a bird's claw may slip forward so that it rests on the perch or floor. In this case, tie the claw back to the leg for a few days with a strip of Cellophane tape or a piece of soft wool; be careful not to restrict the blood flow, otherwise the bird will lose its hind toe.

Lumps is the name given to feather cysts. All birds can suffer from this, even wild varieties, but some of the heavier breeds of canary—such as the Norwich—are more prone to do so than the smaller breeds. This trouble arises from the habit of breeders in the past of trying to obtain more size in their birds by breeding buff to buff, in other words coarse feather to coarse feather, until the feather becomes so large and soft that it cannot pass through the feather follicle; it then turns back inside the skin, forming a cheesy mass that goes on swelling and forming lumps. Eventually the lumps will drop off, but are most unsightly and prevent the bird from being shown. Such birds should never be used for breeding.

Many canaries suffer from **fits**; they will make a cheeping noise and fall to the ground. It is best to leave them alone, since they usually come round quite quickly and show no sign of illness. Some birds will have a fit if they enter a bath or are run into a show cage. There is no cure for this, and so birds with a tendency to have fits must clearly not be placed in such situations. Some birds may also go blind; again there is nothing you can do. Such drawbacks usually arise through inbreeding.

Indigestion covers a number of troubles such as crop-binding, lack of suitable grit or even sour food. The cure is to mix two or three drops of liquid paraffin in the bird's daily portion of seed until there is an improvement.

Loose droppings can be corrected by sprinkling carbonate of bismuth powder over some bread and milk, and continuing this treatment until the droppings become normal again.

The fungus diseases belong to the plant kingdom. **Aspergillosis** attacks the lungs and air sacs; the fungus causes small swellings, usually in the air passage and on the tongue. Symptoms are invariably like those of asthma and bronchitis, but without the gasping sound. This disease is not usually encountered if the cage is kept clean and only fresh food given, but if it does occur two or three drops of tincture of iodine placed in the drinking water may effect a cure if given in the early stages.

Thrush is also usually the result of not keeping the cages clean and of overcrowding. It is found in the crop and intestines. The cure is a teaspoonful of Epsom salts left in the drinking water for 48 hours, combined with scrupulous cleanliness.

7. PARASITES

Unfortunately, birds are prone to a great many parasites. These attack the body and the feathers, some internally, and others externally. Mites and lice are external parasites which are mostly very small but visible to the naked eye. Their life span is between 7 and 21 days, but it is shorter in very warm weather and many of them cannot survive our normal winter. Mites belong to the tick and spider family, but lice—which are very much larger—are insects.

The most common of the mites is the **red mite** (*Dermanyssus*) which attacks the birds at night and sucks their blood. It is actually grey, but the blood of its victims shows through its body so that it appears red. During the hours of daylight it hides in some dark corner such as the end of a perch, any cracks there may be in the cage or even in the seedhopper. A favourite place is the top of the cage if a wooden slide has been left there. These mites are great travellers, and if large numbers are present they can be detected by the quantity of dirty grey spots that they leave around their hideouts.

The **feather mites** are fairly numerous and include *Megnina* which at one time was blamed by Dr Armour for French moult in budgerigars, though this has since been disproved. They enter the feather follicle and make their way to the lungs where they make a permanent home.

Depluming mite (*Knemidokoptes laevis*) or **Scabies** eats into the feather follicle causing intense irritation, so that the bird will often pull out its own feathers. The feathers fall out after a time in any case, and the head is often attacked, causing the bird to go bald. In the past many other complaints, including impetigo and dietary troubles, have been blamed for this. The mite disappears in cold weather.

Quill mites (*Syringophilus*) have also been found in the feather shafts; they gain entrance while the quill is open, before the feather has fully grown.

Scaly leg (*Knemidokoptes mutans*) is a mange mite which causes the legs to grow raised scales. If the legs are gently massaged between the fingers with olive oil, this will kill the mite after a few days and cause the scales to become loose. They will soon come away, but must not be assisted or bleeding will occur.

The **northern mite** (*Ornithonyssus sylviarum*) is brought to Britain by its host the Blackcap (*Sylvia stricapilla*). Usually, the first sign of these pests is when one feels an itching on the face, arms or hands after attending to a cage or touching a nest. By this time there are usually thousands of them all over the nest and cage. Unlike red mites they spend all their time on the host. The irritation is intense, and sometimes after dealing with them one has to strip and bathe to get rid of them. They are usually brought into the birdroom on chickweed, dandelion, etc. If neglected for a few days there will be literally millions of them, but they seem to concentrate on specific areas in the birdroom; while one cage is full of them, perhaps the next two cages may be free and the next under heavy attack. The northern mite turns up in the majority of birdrooms sooner or later, and in nearly every case when young are in the nest. During the autumn, winter and early spring they are not in evidence.

There are also quite a number of different species of lice. They remain on the bird all the time, and it is possible for a bird to have several kinds of lice on its body. The eggs are laid along the feather shafts; some lice suck, while others gnaw the body or feathers. Most young birds about 5 weeks old are attacked by the **feather lice**, which concentrate around the neck and head where the bird is unable to reach them. Many young birds are spoiled for the Young Stock Shows because of this trouble. The **sucking lice** usually appear if the bird is at all below par. I should stress that these pests have nothing to do with cleanliness in the birdroom or the cages, they just appear. The majority of them come out or are much more active in hot weather.

Many people are unaware that the different species of *coccidia* are all parasites, and produce egg-like bodies called 'cocysts' inside the bird. Some cause internal bleeding, and others make the bird weak and very thin so that the breastbone is sharply defined and only just covered with skin. In these cases it is not long before the affected birds die. Other *coccidia* do not cause death, but the bird remains weak and ill. One thing they all have in common is that the 'cocysts' are not active for the first 48 hours, and as the trouble is spread through the birds' eating of infected droppings, the daily cleaning of cages and all cage utensils is imperative, as is a thorough disinfecting of the cages.

A few years ago it was necessary to keep many kinds of cure for mites and lice, including dusting powders. However, all the external mites, including the dreaded northern and red varieties, can now be eliminated by the use of Johnson's 'Anti-Mite'. This is an aerosol spray which is used on the birds direct even when in the nests. A puff or two in the cage will eliminate all known parasites, but it does not kill the eggs of the mites and lice, and therefore several further applications must be given.

8. CAGES AND EQUIPMENT

The metal pet cages sold in most pet shops are suitable for the pet canary. If the perches supplied are round, replace them with the oval type described later. Sand sheets specially sold for the purpose are best for a floor covering. The cage should be covered with a dark cloth at early evening, and it should never be kept near a window where the fluctuations of temperature in such a position will bring on soft moult, explained in Chapter 6.

The only cages that I can recommend for breeding canaries are the box type, which can be singles, doubles or trebles. The top, back, sides and floor are made from wood, and the front is wire with holes through which the birds can reach in order to take seed or water from hoppers hung on the outside of the cage. My own preference is for the double breeding cage. These can be installed right along one side and across the back of the room, while the third side can be fitted with large flight cages. The cages should be placed in metal racks or on brackets attached to the birdroom walls, thus enabling a cage near to or on the bottom of a row to be easily removed for attention and cleaning without disturbing any others. The breeding cages should be about 36 inches long, 16 inches high and 12 inches deep, though these sizes can be varied by a few inches to suit either the room or the birds being kept; the Gloster canary, for instance, does not require such a large cage, and in the case of the Yorkshire variety the height should be at least eighteen inches.

These cages can be divided into two by means of a wire or wooden slide, so that the cock bird can be separated from the hen, or alternatively a breeding hen can be accommodated in each half. Some breeders prefer a tray on the bottom which can be removed for cleaning; others like to have a strip of wood fixed along the front which can be removed by turning two clips, so that the floor covering can be scraped out into a dustbin by a small rake. I have tried both methods, and have no particular preference. The floor covering should be coarse sawdust, as this has many advantages over sand. It is absorbent, and will also act as a cushion if eggs are dropped on the floor by the hen, or if the very small newly hatched chicks are accidentally carried from the nest by the hen's plumage and fall.

A basic aim should be uniformity in all cages and equipment; apart from the workmanlike appearance, a great deal of time and patience will be saved if everything is interchangeable. The inside of the cage should be painted with either an emulsion paint or enamel; most of the modern paints are leadless, which is important. It is also important to use a light-coloured paint, so that the cages can receive the maximum amount of light. I use powder blue, but cream or eau-de-nil will do equally well. The exterior of the cages can be painted black, or better still, with one of the proprietary wood preservatives which can now be obtained in a variety of colours. The wire parts should also be painted black.

Perches should be oval and made of soft wood. There are several methods of fixing these, and it is essential that they do not twist, otherwise faulty mating can take place. After trying many different ways, there is no doubt in my mind that the best type is the one shown in the sketch. This type can be changed in a second if all the wire fronts are interchangeable as suggested above, and can also be removed from the outside. Furthermore, there is a certain amount of up-and-down movement which is kind to the birds' feet, but could not adversely affect mating. The size of the perches can be altered to suit your birds, as can the shape, provided the square section fitting is constant.

Drinking vessels can be of a number of different types; the glass 'hat' drinker is very popular, but I prefer the larger 'jumbo' type which is better with the flight cages. Seedhoppers vary in size and shape, but I have found the one illustrated to be most satisfactory; it has the largest seed capacity where it is needed. Some small jars will be required to contain grit—little round fishpaste pots are ideal for the purpose. For fixing cuttlefish bone the holder illustrated is most suitable. It can be made in a minute or two from a piece of cage wire, and fixed on the wooden rail into which the cage front fits. Hang-on baths are another necessity, and can be purchased from most bird shops. I will deal with other accessories in the appropriate chapters.

Although I have advocated double breeders, nevertheless both the treble and single varieties have their advantages. Should large flight cages be unsuitable for any reason, then the treble cages with both slides removed make a good substitute. If there is enough space, it is a good plan to have a row of single cages in the birdroom; they can house the odd cock when a double breeder is being used for two hens, and will also make good weaning cages. Their size should be about 18 inches long by 16 inches high and 12 inches deep, but—as I have already pointed out—these sizes can be altered to suit the room. If you are handy with carpentry tools you can make these breeding cages quite easily; the fronts can be made from punch bar and 14-gauge wire, or can be ordered to your own specifications from the manufacturers.

If you are doing the work yourself, keep the cages as simple as possible. A plain box with a wire front is all that is required; artistic scrolls, fancy mouldings and so on make certain hideouts for mites.

Two other items of equipment which should be in the birdroom are a fine sieve (about 10-inch will be large enough) and a metal strainer (a gravy strainer is ideal). The former is for sieving the seed and the latter for cleaning the soaked seed.

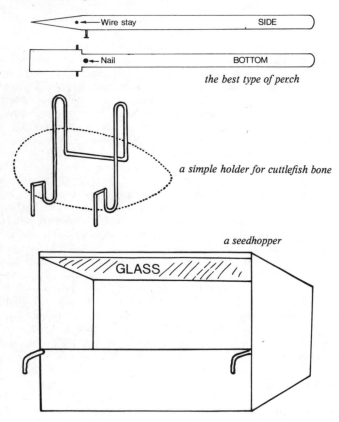

the best type of perch

a simple holder for cuttlefish bone

a seedhopper

GLASS

9. PREPARING FOR THE BREEDING SEASON

The right preparation for the breeding season is very important indeed. Preparation of the birds should start at the end of the year; it is useless only to begin thinking about breeding a week or two before the birds are going to be paired up. In my opinion, no hens should be shown after Christmas; they should be allowed to settle down comfortably in the birdroom for the trying months of January, February and March.

Soft food should be started during the winter and gradually increased as the breeding season approaches. My own food consists of hard-boiled eggs, finely sieved and mixed with ordinary oatmeal, the latter being used in the same bulk proportion as the egg; no water is needed, as there is sufficient moisture in the egg to make the mass crumbly. (This food was accidentally discovered by Mr D. W. Dawson, the well-known Yorkshire canary breeder. He thought he had a spare bag of the food he had previously been mixing with the eggs, but was mistaken; it was a Sunday morning—no chance of buying anything in the shops—and when he spotted a packet of Scots oatmeal in the larder he decided to use it with the eggs. Later on he found that every bit of this food had been eaten and obviously enjoyed by the birds. Since that day he has used no other soft food for conditioning and rearing, and several of his friends (myself included) regard it as the find of the century as regards canary feeding.) I also add a dessertspoonful of Glucose D to this food. There is no need to give clipped oats or groats now as these are included in this soft food. If you are using my suggested seed mixture, niger seed is also being fed daily and there is no requirement for this to be given separately.

When I first kept canaries I was quite convinced that the best way to feed was the natural way, and had very little time for the manufactured supplements that were advertised. Possibly I was right in those days, but now I have altered my views. Unfortunately most foods are prepared in a way that is far from natural and have not got the real nutrient value of former days; therefore I now add a little of these vitamin powders to my soft food.

About the beginning of March, one should examine the birds' feet and beaks and, if necessary, clip them back to normal size. To trim the claws, hold the bird's leg up to a strong light and you will see where the bloodstream finishes in each claw. Using a sharp pair of scissors, or nail clippers, cut just in front of the dark line which is the bloodstream. This will cause a slight shock to the birds, but there is plenty of time for them to recover before breeding commences. I usually carry out this task as I place the hens in their particular breeding cage. Some breeders also give the birds a hand wash at this time, but I do not think this necessary unless the birds are kept in a built-up area where they get really dirty. In February it is a good plan to have a really good 'spring-clean' in the birdroom; all the cages should be thoroughly washed out with soap and water to which a good disinfectant has been added, and they can if necessary be repainted and any damage to the wire, etc., repaired.

February is also about the latest time to obtain new stock. October should be the target month for this, but often some of the 'hens' turn out to be cocks, or one or two may not have come through the winter too well, so that an additional bird or two is required. The chances of a hen settling down and breeding in a strange environment under another management after February are not too bright, but I have known exceptional cases where hens introduced in April had chicks by May.

There are a number of articles that you will need for successful breeding, and it is best to order these early so that all are to hand when required. Firstly, you will need nest pans—allow two per breeding pair. These can be the ordinary round earthenware variety, the round basket-type or small square open boxes with perforated zinc bottoms. I have tried all of them with a fair amount of success, but now use the old-type earthenware nest pan as it is easier to clean and there are no crevices to harbour mites, etc. If you decide to use these pans you will require nest felts; these fit inside the pan and can be dark felt or white (the latter are known as swansdown and are dea er). Once again I have no particular preference. There are holes in the nest pan to which the felts can be stitched, but I prefer to stick mine with carbolic soap. I buy a tablet of this very cheap soap, place it in an old cocoa tin or something similar, add a little water and heat the tin on a stove. This makes the soap temporarily liquid, and the felt can be pasted in the pan with a brush; not only does it stick well but also it acts as a very good deterrent to red mites. I have been using my present tin for four years.

You will also need metal pan holders to hang on the side or back of the cage from a small hook. Nesting material is essential; I use medical tow as it is very cheap and ideal for the purpose. A few dried grasses and a little moss should also be offered. Split rings are a 'must' to indicate the young birds. Do not rely on your memory—I know from past experience that this can let you down, especially if you have bred a number of clear birds. The rings can be of different colours or two colours to a ring. Some fanciers prefer one particular colour for each year, and in this case the rings are numbered.

This brings me to an item which is a most important point in the canary room. You must register each bird and put down all relevant details as to breeding, parentage, number of eggs laid, fecundity and how the young have been ringed.

Dummy eggs must also be purchased: these are substituted for the real eggs and I will refer to them again in the following chapter. A small cabinet or container is also required to store the real eggs. The cages should be numbered, and an easy way to do this is to cut out the digits on an out-of-date calendar and stick the numbers on the appropriate cages. Alternatively, the numbers can be painted on the cages. Also order a plunger feeder, as this may save a promising youngster or two if the parents stop feeding after a week or two. You can use nesting material racks which fit on the outside of the cage, but I prefer simply to stick this material between the existing wires. Most important is an aerosol insect spray, but I have discussed this at greater length in Chapter 7.

Needless to say, you will make sure that you have a sufficient supply of foods, seeds, etc., to last for the whole of the breeding season. The last item required is a hospital cage, and this can be of the utmost importance, especially if a hen is suffering from egg-binding. Many of the textbooks advise giving the hens Epsom salts and cutting down on their extra foods, if they are a little fat, in order to prevent egg-binding, but I do not believe in this at all. I like to see a little fat on my hens at the start of the breeding season, as they have a long and tiring time ahead of them and a little something in reserve is all to the good. I have not had one case of egg-binding in my room for over 15 years. In nine cases out of ten, chills are the cause of egg-binding; warmth is the answer, and this is where the hospital cage is invaluable.

10. THE BREEDING SEASON

It has been said that there are more ways of breeding canaries than there are days in the year, and I would not disagree with this. I have known of highly successful breedings achieved by rearing on currant buns, turkey pellets, wild seeds, bread and milk, soaked seed and carrot, and many more unlikely things. I encountered one of the strangest breedings of all some years ago when visiting Mr P. W. Butler. A boy knocked at his door and, enquiring if he could sex some young canaries, produced a small round wire pet cage in which were four young birds and their parents. Mr Butler explained that it was most difficult to sex young canaries, but he would make an attempt. He asked the lad where the birds had been bred: 'In this cage,' was the reply. Further questioning revealed that no nest pan or nesting materials had been provided; the hen had laid four eggs in the sand at the bottom of the cage and had hatched them all out. No rearing food had been supplied: just the usual packet seed and a dandelion leaf! I thought of some of my own pampered birds which had failed to rear a chick!

This event did, however, help to confirm what I have always maintained: that nine out of ten successful breedings depend upon both birds being 100 per cent breeding fit. I am still convinced that this is the real secret of success. I am sure the hens deceive us by calling for the cock, making a nest and laying eggs when they are not really at the peak of condition, and I believe that nothing less is good enough. Looking back over nearly half a century, I cannot recall one British breeder who has put down a dozen pairs of canaries and had every pair lay and rear. There may have been exceptions, but they are few and far between. A well-known Yorkshire breeder, with one of the best birdrooms in the country, had spared no expense in ensuring that conditions were first class when he put down about 80 pairs, yet he told me that the average number of young from these high-class Yorkshires was $1\frac{1}{2}$ birds per pair. I am satisfied if I breed an average of 3 birds per pair. I do not want to dishearten the tyro—far from it—and I am only referring to high-class pedigree stock. Many Gloster, Border and Lizard breeders average well over 5 per pair, but even then some birds will rear 8 or 9 chicks and others none.

I suppose this uncertainty is one of the main attractions of the Fancy. It certainly presents a challenge, and if canary breeding were as simple as breeding white mice, it would lose much of its appeal and the canary would be of little value.

By February the hens should be in their selected cages, while the cocks should be separated by the wire slide in the double breeder and singing lustily. Some breeders tie a piece of coarse string from the top rail over the perch, for the hen to pull about. Most textbooks state that the birds should be ready for breeding by the first week in April. This, in my opinion, has been the prime cause of so many failures in the past, and I would re-emphasise that the time for breeding is when the birds are fully fit. This may be in March, or more likely in May, depending upon the weather, winter management and the amount of artificial light and heat used. Many beginners are also misled by seeing the hen dashing up and down with a piece of material or feather in her beak. I like to see this for it shows that things are progressing in the right way, but it does not mean that the bird is 100 per cent breeding fit. When the material is held right back between the mandibles, as far as possible, it is a good sign. A reliable test for fitness in the hen is to hang a singing cock (in a show cage) on the outside of her cage. Any cock will do for this purpose; if the hen immediately squats, flutters her wings and calls for mating, you can consider her about ready. The cock, if fully fit, will pull himself right out of shape and sing lustily while lifting his feet one after the other from the perch as if it was red hot. I like to introduce the nest pan to the hen before the cock, and if she is ready she should make a nest within a few days. For the beginner, I advise one cock to each hen, and they should be left together all the time. In later years the hen can be allowed to rear on her own, and the cock can be used with two or even three hens. but it takes a little experience to know exactly when to replace the cock. If he persistently worries the hen, then of course he must be removed. I think one of the prettiest sights is to see a nest of four or five young being fed, simultaneously, by the cock and the hen perched each side of the nest.

The night before the first egg is laid, it is quite possible that the hen may be looking a bit 'thick'. Unflighted hens are more prone to this than their elder sisters. If when you go into the birdroom the following morning the hen is all fluffed up, and is on the bottom of the cage, she is most likely egg-bound. Do not hesitate: place her in a hospital cage and raise the temperature to 30°C (90°F). In an hour or so the egg should be expelled. If you have not got such a cage, fix a rubber hot-water bottle in the bottom of a single breeder or another small cage (a bird-bath will do, with the open side filled in). Cover the bottle with some flannel so that the bird will not get burned, and place the cage in front of the fire or in the warmest place possible. In nine out of ten cases this will do the trick. Normally the egg will be laid in the nest before you pay your first visit to the birdroom in the morning, and you should remove it straight away and replace it with a dummy. Some writers think this is unnecessary, especially on the first round. I have tried leaving the eggs as laid, and in most cases have had the mortification of losing the last one or two chicks to be hatched, as the first birds to arrive were far too strong and the later ones died because they could not compete for food. Great care must be taken of the eggs. I have a small wooden cabinet in my room, the drawers of which I have divided into some 20 squares; each square is numbered, and eggs are placed in the drawer bearing the number of the cage from which they are taken. All the squares are half filled with sawdust. A box would serve the same purpose, but be sure that it cannot fall or get knocked over, as this could be a tragedy and the valuable eggs would be spoiled.

As a rule a number of hens will 'go down' (start laying) at about the same time. Another advantage of removing the eggs, therefore, is that you can wait a few days and put down several birds together. This has the great merit that if one of the hens does not feed, or if only one chick is hatched out, a bit of swopping can take place and perhaps a valuable chick can be saved. I prefer to set my hens in the evening. I remove the dummies and replace them with the real eggs on the third night. Some hens make a bad nest, and in this case I make one for them. An old electric light bulb is ideal for rounding the interior surface of the nest after you have built it up with the nesting material. Directly you have set the hen, make a note in the bird register of the date when they are due to hatch. I add 13 days to the date on which the eggs were set, and although I am often a day too soon I feel this is preferable to being a day late and having no soft food for the young on the first morning. Quite a number of breeders advocate giving the sitting hen only plain canary seed, or at the most canary seed and a little rape seed. I myself carry on with the same food as before, including a little green food, since I can see no valid reason for altering the birds' diet. A number of breeders test the eggs during the sitting period, by holding them up to a strong light to see whether or not they are clear. I feel there is no point in this, especially for the novice. When the hen goes broody she has what amounts to a mild form of fever; her body temperature rises and this causes her to brood. It is best to allow her to go the full cycle of laying and brooding: nothing is accomplished by removing the eggs at 7 or 8 days.

On the evening of the thirteenth day, place a little soft food in the cage—I do mean a little, just enough to cover a shilling. The beginner must exercise a lot of patience at this time, and resist the urge to turn the hen off the nest in order to see how many chicks have been hatched. Such action will only cause her to sit very tight, and she may not leave the nest to feed the young but allow the cock to feed her while she keeps the young well down and squashed in the nest. I break all the rules here by giving the birds a few sprigs of seeding chickweed. This usually entices the hen off the nest, and enables me to have a peep. All the textbooks advise no green food of any kind until the third day, but for many years I have given my birds a little chickweed from the first day, and as far as I know have never lost a chick by doing so. After all, it is a natural food, and if the hen were in the wild she would not find egg food waiting for her. I am convinced that the secret of successful rearing is to give very small portions of food as often as possible. This tempts the hen off the nest, and each time she returns there are hungry little mouths awaiting her. The babies require very little food for the first day or two, and over-generous amounts of soft foods given to the parents can cause them to become satiated and lose interest in feeding. I am aware that if one is away all day food has to be left for a long period, but even then leave as little as possible, and if your wife is at home prevail upon her to give a midday feed of bread and milk and a late afternoon feed of egg food. You can see to the other things when you return from work. The soaked seed is given from the third day.

If for some reason your hens are not feeding, but your pal Jack's birds are doing well on some other kind of soft food, on no account switch right over to this diet. You must carry on with the food to which your birds have become accustomed, though you can of course try tempting the hen to feed with such things as chickweed, dandelion heads or different soaked seeds. I had a Norwich hen that refused to feed with anything but dandelion heads. I used to pack the chicks with soft food by hand every night, but I am not convinced that my attentions made any difference. As a rule the hen will feed the usual soft food once the chicks become large and strong.

Fix a perch each side and just above the nest to make sure that the hen does not fly straight out and in so doing carry out one of the chicks. Should this occur in any case, and you see what appears to be a tiny lifeless form on the floor, do not despair, but place it in your partially closed hand and breathe warm air on to it for a few minutes. In nearly every case you will feel it start to wriggle after a while, then you can replace it in the nest.

After a few days it may appear that one of the hens is sweating. In the old days, the advice for dealing with this trouble was to transfer the chicks to a wooden box with a perforated zinc bottom, so that the hen could cool down. Today we know that birds have no sweat glands: they expel heat through the mouth like a dog. This so-called 'sweating' is caused by the chicks being off colour, having been fed some stale food which has upset them; their excreta, which at this early age are encased in a transparent bag and removed by the parents (to be either swallowed or dropped over the side of the nest), become very liquid and cause the little bag to burst. These sticky liquid excreta go all over the hen's breast and feathers, giving her this sweating appearance, and also cover the little head fluff of the chicks, plastering it down and making them look very bedraggled. By all means, transfer them all to another nest. The cure is to place a teaspoonful of Epsom salts in the drinking water, so that the hen has a good clean-out. In the event of this trouble, it is also best to stop the egg food and give bread and milk to which a generous amount of glucose has been added. Continue with the egg food when the trouble is over. If all goes well, remove the young birds into a weaning cage when they are 21 days old, either a single breeder or half a double breeder. I consider the 21-day interval very important, for if left later the young birds seem to take a great deal of weaning. In any case they will interfere with the hen, who should start laying in the new nest you have provided. If the hen should start to strip the feathers from the young birds after about 16 days or so, transfer the nest to the other side of the double breeder, using the wire slide, and the cock will feed and rear the young ones. This is another advantage of keeping the cock and hen together all the time when breeding.

When you start to wean the young birds, you should place a ring on their legs. I usually place the ring on the right leg for the first round, and on the left leg for the second. When you buy your rings a small instrument will be given to you, free, for this purpose. The next thing is to write in the register the details of the birds ringed, and the colour and number of the rings.

Prepare your cage beforehand. I cut up a dozen pieces of newspaper to fit the tray or bottom of the cage. You can use a feeding board, which consists of a small wooden tray; the front part goes under the cage door, and at the rear there is a leg to keep it level with the door. In the middle of this board, place some milk sop over which you have sprinkled some maw seed. As a general rule the youngsters will peck at the black spots which are the maw seed, then get the taste for the food. Sometimes, however, they will just sit and cry for the parents to feed them, in which case you should gently wipe the beak of one bird in the milk sop. It will then taste the food, and once it begins to feed all the others will soon follow. *Do not*, and I must emphasise this, *do not* get worried if they continue to cry for the parents, and do not put the young back with them; if you do, you will have endless troubles. I know that this is a trying time for the beginner, but I can state that all over the years I have never lost any young which were 21 days old through starvation.

Remove one layer of newspaper every morning, and you can see by the birds' droppings how things are progressing. On the third day, when the birds are picking up their food satisfactorily, I fix a thin soft wood perch about 4 inches up, and on about the ninth day I fix another about 8 inches high. This perching is to prevent slip claw, to which I have referred in an earlier chapter. When the birds are weaned, fill the seedhopper with red rape only. The water pots should have been on all the time, and although it will be some little while before they eat the seed or drink the water, it is ready for them when they do want it. On the third day I give them the egg food, and about the fourth or fifth day, the soaked seed and a few sprigs of chickweed or a dandelion leaf. After the seventh day, a bath is provided on all suitable days. When I find they are cracking the rape seed well, I change to the basic seed and place a pot of grit in the cage. This is the time when—in the past—many of the young birds have 'gone light'. This is a wasting disease which seems to attack them when they have gone on to seed. Since I started using plenty of Glucose D my birds have never suffered from this complaint, and provided the birds and the cage are kept very clean, I see no reason why it should occur.

The birds will also want training at this time, but more of this later. If possible I like to wean about 4 or 5 birds together, but when they are about 5 weeks old they should be separated and placed two in a cage. The main reason for this is that if a number of young birds are kept together, sooner or later one will pull out a feather from one of its companions, take a liking to the juicy end of the quill and develop a taste for it; before you know what is happening, most of the birds will have been deprived of their feathers. Worse still, you will have feather-pluckers in your birdroom. When the young birds are about 12 to 14 weeks old they will break into their first moult, and most of your trials and tribulations during the breeding season are over. Do not take more than two rounds from any hen, and do not allow another round to start in July.

I have described my own method of breeding canaries, and this has been well tested over the years. If the reader intends to start breeding canaries, or has not had much success hitherto, I fully recommend that he carries out my procedure. I cannot guarantee success, but I can say that for very many years I have not had a hen egg-bound, young 'going light', a sweating hen or any red mites. I have had bad years, but I have always managed to breed a number of good birds. If the reader is already breeding successfully, then I advise him to stick to his own method and on no account to change. I have tried to explain breeding of canaries in as plain and straightforward a manner as possible. We could have explored many side lanes, but in all probability this would only have confused the main issue.

Towards the end of July, the annual moult takes place. Some of the young birds bred early in the year will have already started to moult. This is a very trying time for the stock. The over-year birds will lose all their feathers and have to regrow a complete set from their own body. Birds bred in the current year do not lose their flight or tail feathers, and are known as unflighted, or in some parts of the country as non-flights. I imagine this is Nature's way of allowing these inexperienced birds to retain the full power of flight as a protection against predators. For those varieties requiring colour-feeding, a little sweet red pepper should be added to the soft food. Carophyll Red is a substance now being used by some breeders; this is a very strong colour medium which if used incorrectly will ruin the birds' colour for showing, so my advice to the novice is to stick to the recognised medium at first and to experiment with this colour when he has a number of birds to spare after a successful breeding season. Many birds on the show bench have a brilliant colour. The late Walter Turner, a well-known Norwich canary breeder, used to show yellow cocks that were described in the report of the show as 'balls of fire'. I well remember at one of the early National Shows, another well-known Norwich fancier saying to Walter, 'I will give you £100 for your secret of colour feeding,' but Walter only laughed. Later he said to me that he could have had the 'secret' for nothing. Firstly, you must breed for colour, and secondly, you must start colour-feeding before any feathers begin to fall. The textbooks state that you should start to colour-feed when the birds commence to drop their feathers, but this is too late. You will of course have partial success, but never 100 per cent.

As already stated, this is a very trying time for the birds and many are ruined for life at this stage. They should be given all the extras possible. I like to give shepherd's purse at this time. I am very keen on this weed, and when I kept rabbits I found it a wonderful cure for the scours. I do not know if it has the same effect on birds, but I can say that when I have used it my birds have not suffered from loose droppings. I have heard of some cases where moving the cage from one part of the room to another has caused the birds to die, also of others where merely running them into show cages has resulted in death. I have always thought there might be some other reason for this, but I may be wrong. In any case it cannot be emphasised too much that the birds should be interfered with as little as possible during the moulting period. The aim is for a quick moult, and if birds are moved about or disturbed in any way, then it is likely that they will become what is known as 'stuck in the moult'. This condition can last for many months, and more often than not develops into pulmonary trouble. The moult takes about 12 to 14 weeks if all goes well.

As I have stated, the 'secret' of good colour-feeding is to begin some time before the bird starts to moult. Start by mixing a little colour in the food, just enough to colour it slightly, and then gradually increase the colour until it forms 20 per cent of the whole. The reason for this is that the bird is likely to refuse it if confronted with a different-looking food—it must be slowly accustomed to it. I feed the colour food for six days, then give bread and milk plus the Glucose D on the seventh day. I continue in this way until the end of the moult, and then give the colour food two or three times a week for the rest of the show season—say, up to December. Once again, I must impress upon the novice that only small portions of colour food are required; at this moulting period the ends of the quills are open, and the bloodstream flows into the feather. It is the function of the colour food to colour the blood, and one can appreciate that it does not take a great deal of colour to do this and to maintain it; enough to cover a sixpence is sufficient per bird. The blood can only absorb so much, after which the bird will get rid of the excess colour in its excreta; when these come out bright red you know that you are overfeeding the colour food. For those birds that are not colour-fed, I still advocate continuing with the soft food and giving plenty of green food, which will improve the colour in a natural manner. All possible wild foods should also be given, including chickweed, charlock, knotgrass, plantain, sow-thistle, dock, thistle and many more. Many breeders favour nasturtium leaves, and some even give the red flowers. Even after all these years I am still very glad when the moult has finished, and the cages and birdroom are no longer smothered with feathers. The last part of a bird to moult is its face and head. Sometimes in the young birds a few light feathers in the face, showing where they have not moulted, will persist for some weeks after the rest of the bird has completed the process.

1 Serin Finch

2 Clear Norwich Yellow Unflighted Cock

3 Clear Norwich Buff Hen

4 Cinnamon Buff Cock

5 Cinnamon Buff Hen

6 Clear Yorkshire Yellow Unflighted Cock

7 Clear Yorkshire Buff Hen

8 Wing-marked Yorkshire Buff Cock

9 Eye- Wing- Tail-marked Yorkshire Yellow Hen

10 Self-Green Yorkshire Cock

11 Clear Border Yellow Cock

12 Clear Border Buff Hen

13 Clear and Variegated White Border

14 Self-Blue and Self-Fawn Borders

15 Self-Green Border Yellow Cock

16 Self-Cinnamon Border

17 Eye- Wing- Tail-marked Border

18 Gloster Corona

19 Gloster Consort

20 Tail- Wing-marked Gloster Corona

21 Self-Green Gloster Consort

22 Red Orange

23 Hooded Siskin

24 Apricot

25 Rose Pastel

26 Copper Hybrid

27 Ivory Pastel

28 Clear-capped Gold Lizard

29 Clear-capped Silver Lizard

30 Noncapped Gold Lizard Hen

31 Broken-capped Silver Lizard Hen

32 Scotch Fancy

33 Frill

34 Crest

35 Variegated Crest-bred Hen

36 Lancashire Coppy

37 Lancashire Plainhead

38 Belgian Fancy

39 Fife Fancy

40 London Fancy

41 Clear Goldfinch × Canary

42 Clear Greenfinch × Canary

43 Clear Goldfinch × Eye- Wing-marked Canary

44 Dark Linnet × Canary

45 Canary × Bullfinch

46 Siskin × Canary

47 Dark Goldfinch × Canary

48 Dark Greenfinch × Canary

THE EXHIBITION CANARY

INTRODUCTION

In Chapter 2 I advised the beginner to go to one breeder only so that he could obtain birds that were line-bred. Line or pedigree breeding is essential to continuing success on the show bench. This means pairing cousins, uncles to nieces, aunts to nephews, perhaps father to daughter, but in only the most exceptional cases brother to sister. The advantage of this type of breeding is that you perpetuate the good points in your birds, but you can do likewise with bad features; so it is essential to have the right stock from the start and to be ruthless in eliminating all birds carrying such faults. Once again this emphasises the importance of the register.

All canaries—and indeed all birds—are termed either yellow or buff; the old-time fanciers' words for these were jonque and mealy. These terms have nothing to do with colour—a blackbird can be yellow or a buff—but they refer to the texture of the feather. The yellow is a fine silky feather and the buff is coarse with a whitish edge known as mealing; so the old-time fanciers' word was in my opinion the best for this kind of bird. Yellow and buff can be compared with true blonde and brunette in human beings, one having fine hair and the other coarse. Most yellow hens seem to carry a little mealing, and there are cases where it is difficult to decide if they are yellow or buff, but these are the exceptions. Once I bred a Yorkshire that was yellow on one side and buff on the other, so that it appeared a different bird, depending upon the side from which it was viewed. It is essential to pair yellow to buff; if you pair yellow to yellow you will obtain small birds with small heads, while buff to buff will produce coarse-feathered birds. I should point out that it is feather which makes the exhibition bird. Some years ago in the United States, a large number of Norwich canary skulls were measured with the latest measuring device, and it was found that the skulls did not vary by one-thousandth part of an inch; yet before the feathers were removed some of these birds appeared to have large broad heads, while those of others seemed small and snipey. Most varieties of canary can be found in different colours—green, cinnamon and white. There are also the clear birds which carry no variegation; these can be green-ground birds or cinnamons, the latter only being distinguished by their red eyes. The greens can be self-green, variegated or carry a small mark known as a tick; to make it more confusing, such birds can also be cinnamon carriers. It is best to pair a marked bird to a clear if suitable, since this should produce clears, lightly marked or variegated young. If too many marked birds are being produced, you can pair clear to clear; this should result in a majority of clears. Many fanciers have slipped up in the past by concentrating on clear to clear, and have found after a few generations that they have lost both size and colour. It is essential at times to have a 'dip in the green' as it is called.

Whites can also be clear or variegated, and some carry a tinge of yellow. These white birds are not albinos, and from them can be bred fawns and blues. The white canary should be paired to a normal—it does not matter if it is a buff or a yellow. Should the dominant whites be paired together the effect on 25 per cent of the young will be lethal. The expected results of such a mating would be 50 per cent of dominant whites, 25 per cent of normal yellow ground and 25 per cent of non-viable dominant whites; in other words, one in every four chicks will not survive.

The blues are really a slatey colour and represent the green blood, while the fawns represent the cinnamon blood. Cinnamons, like all birds, are either yellows or buffs, but the cinnamon feather is usually finer than the normal feather and this is important in some varieties, such as the Yorkshire, where a large bird with good feather is required. This breeding point must be watched, however, otherwise the birds will finish up too small and with snipey heads. Nevertheless, some of the best birds seen on the show bench have been cinnamons.

Training for exhibitions is extremely important in regard to the type canaries, and should be started when the birds are about 5 weeks old and have begun to pick up hard seed. Hanging the show cage on the outside of the stock-cage door is the method to adopt, for the birds will soon hop in and find their way on to the perches. Showing is bred into them, but this early training is essential. I have known canaries which have been placed in an outdoor aviary for over 12 months following early training; however, when placed in a show cage again they have immediately worked the perches like good show birds.

One golden rule is never to show a bird unless it is 100 per cent fit. This is a great temptation to the novice when an important show is due and he has entered his best bird, but when he runs it in the show cage the night before he finds it is not quite fit. He may think that, as the weather is cold and the show hall is warm, the bird will perhaps be all right later, but no judge will consider a bird that is not in top condition, and in most cases the bird will end up by being seriously ill and perhaps ruined for the following breeding season. Also, be sure to place the drinker on their show cages when training birds; I have seen birds become ill at shows because they could not find the drinking water.

Make sure that the show cage is in excellent condition; a good picture is worth a good frame and a shabby show cage could cost you a premier award. I well remember judging a class of over 40 buff Norwich cocks at one of the early National Shows just after the Second World War. I had sorted them all out and finished with two grand birds that I really could not separate. Then I found that one of the cages was dirty and required painting, so I awarded the red ticket to the other to take this large class; it went on to take 'best canary' at this great show. One rather important matter is to study the show schedule in detail, making sure that your birds are entered in the right class. If in doubt consult another fancier. I know this may seem very elementary, but every year there are hundreds of birds wrongly classed at various shows all over the country. It is most frustrating and disappointing to go to the Show or receive the birds back from the Show and find 'W.C.' marked on your cage.

THE NORWICH CANARY
Plates 2, 3

Known as the John Bull of the Fancy, the Norwich was at the height of its popularity during the nineteenth century, when close on 70 birds in one class was not unknown at the larger shows such as the Crystal Palace. It would seem that these birds were originally bred by the Flemish weavers in the sixteenth century; when many of them fled to England to escape the persecutions of the Spanish aggressor, they brought their canaries with them and settled down in and around Norwich in Norfolk. East Anglia has been the stronghold of the Norwich Canary over the centuries, but in more recent years Leicestershire (particularly Hinckley and Burbage) has been very much to the fore. In those early days colour was the main objective and in the early 1870s a furore arose because some birds exhibited were a rich orange colour instead of the usual yellow. Protests were lodged, and the birds were sent to the Public Analyst who could find no artificial colouring in the plumage. Some judges accepted these birds while others disqualified them, until in 1873 it was disclosed that they had been colour-fed on cayenne pepper. This was discovered accidentally, so the story goes, by a fancier who had a Norwich with a chill during the moulting period and thought that a little hot cayenne pepper might cure it. Following this disclosure a rather chaotic period ensued; some shows put on classes for 'Non-fed' and for 'Fed' birds, but a little sharp practice soon put a stop to this since some breeders gave 'just a little' colour food and it was difficult to separate the sheep from the goats. Many fanciers also considered that the hot pepper caused deterioration in the digestive system. When, however, tasteless pepper was tried and found successful, most of the difficulties were solved and colour-fed birds became the only ones catered for at the shows. The trend, however, was to add a little cayenne pepper to the tasteless variety with the idea that it made the colour 'hotter'; this idea persisted right up to the 1930s but is no longer followed.

Round about the time that the colour food was discovered the Crested canary breeders introduced the Lancashire Coppy into their breed, and this was by far the largest variety. The Norwich breeders followed suit, and the Norwich then became known as the Norwich Plainhead to distinguish it from the crested bird. This cross produced coarse feather and completely altered the original Norwich. Following the First World War there was a craze for size, and double buffing became the rule; the birds then came to resemble the Crested breed, with ragged feathers, laying on top of the perch and of course a considerable incidence of the 'lumps'. Many fanciers became disgusted and gave up keeping the Norwich; it looked as if the breed would disappear altogether, a sad thought after it had been the leading canary for so many years. After the Second World War, however, the late Mr A. W. Smith came to the rescue, supported by a number of exhibitors and judges, including myself. All the feathery monstrosities were out, any birds with 'lumps' were out, and indeed if Mr Smith had any suspicions about a bird he would remove it from the show cage and examine it in his hands. As can be imagined this was not very popular in some quarters, but we all supported him and it was not long before these birds were conspicuous by their absence. I can now reveal that Mr Smith used good-quality Borders to cross with his Norwich birds, and after a few generations he succeeded in producing the type of Norwich we were all seeking. Mr Smith was elected President of the

Southern Norwich Plainhead Club, and I am proud to have the honour of being its first Honorary Life Vice-President.

The present-day Norwich is a grand bird, and its popularity would seem to be on the increase judging by the well-filled classes at the National Show. It is not so easy to breed as some of the smaller varieties, and is not a cheap bird to acquire, fair birds fetching from £15 to £20 per pair. Of course birds can be obtained for much less, but it is best to go to a known breeder and buy an unflighted pair. Good show birds will fetch as much as £60, and many change hands at £100, but do not let this put you off if you have a liking for the Norwich; as stated in a previous chapter, you may easily breed such a bird from your £15 pair if obtained from a reliable breeder. If you are successful in this, do not be tempted to sell it but keep it for your own stud.

In my very wide experience of the Fancy I have known all types of fanciers covering all the different birds both British and foreign, and I can say without prejudice that over the years I have found the Norwich fancier second to none when it comes to good sportsmanship and kindness. There is always a good market for the Norwich. Even the inferior birds, not good enough for show, are snapped up by the mule breeders who can never obtain sufficient hens for their purpose.

As the name John Bull implies, it is a thickset bird and should be 'round' all over; a good round head is essential, a mean or 'shield-shaped' head is out. Other features to be looked for are a good deep chest, a short broad back, compact wings, good carriage, a well-packed short tail and a short neat beak. Although not so sprightly as the Border, it should nevertheless stand well off the perch and move freely. The model shows a bold yet clear eye; this should always be aimed for, but a little 'browiness' is usually very hard to eliminate and it should not penalise the bird too much. Some writers advocate keeping a few Borders or other small canaries as feeders for the Norwich. In my opinion this is not at all necessary, but is a retrograde step which if continued will eventually breed a race of non-feeding birds. Most of the leading Norwich men have no other types of bird in their room and find no difficulty in breeding these fine canaries.

There are quite a number of good greens about which are very attractive, but not many whites. Some years ago I came into possession of a very good white cock, and thought I would introduce it into my stock and breed a few whites. Directly I placed it in my room all the birds within sight went berserk, and I could not get a hen to settle down in the same cage as this white. This experience proved to my satisfaction that the so-called expert ornithologists who claimed that birds were colour-blind were quite wrong.

The Norwich does not require a great deal of training, the show on stock cage method is sufficient. The show cage is of the box type, black outside with an interior of Valspar 'Meadow Green'. There is no feeding trough, and the floor covering should be plain canary seed. The drinker is black. The Official Standard is as follows:

		Points
Type	Short and cobby. Back broad and well filled in, showing a slight rise transversely. Chest broad and deep, giving an expansive curved front, and sweeping under therefrom in one full curve to the tail. Ideal length 6–6¼ inches. Stance or position at an angle of about 45 degrees.	25
Head	Proportionately bold and assertive in its carriage. A full forehead rising from a short neat beak. To be well rounded over and across the skull. Cheeks full and clean featured, eye to be well placed and unobscured.	10
Neck	Short and thick, continuing to run from the back skull on to the shoulders, and from a full throat into the breast.	10
Wings	Short and well braced, meeting nicely at the tips to rest lightly, yet closely, on the rump.	10
Tail	Short, closely packed and well filled in at the root. Rigidly carried, giving an all-of-one-piece appearance with the body.	5
Legs and feet	Well set back. Feet perfect.	5
Condition	In full bloom of perfect health. Bold and bouncing movement.	10
Quality of feather	Close and fine in texture, presenting the smooth, silky plumage necessary to give a clean-cut contour.	10
Colour	Rich, bright and level throughout, with sheen or brilliancy. Yellows a deep orange. Buffs rich in ground colour and well mealed.	10
Staging	Clean and correctly staged.	5
		100

THE CINNAMON CANARY
Plates 4, 5

The present-day Cinnamon resembles the Norwich and is a very handsome bird, although when first produced it was a very ordinary canary called the 'Dun'. Cinnamons have had a very chequered history over the past 30 years. Before the First World War they were quite popular and the Specialist Society—the Cinnamon Canary Club—was thriving. After the war there were very few left, and in fact at the first post-war London Inter-Club Show held, where eight classes were given for these birds, only two turned up. Since then there has been a revival, mainly due to Mr W. Henley, his daughter Mrs Peggy Winser and Mr E. O. Winser in the London area; to one or two fanciers in Norwich; and in Suffolk to Mr A. W. Barnes who has been pre-eminent with this variety over the past few years, and who breeds quite a number of first class birds every year.

The main objective with the Cinnamon is to breed trueness of colour. The jonque or yellow must not show any trace or tinge of green, nor any drabness; the stripes on the back should be as faint as possible, and the cinnamon colour must be good and even throughout. The mealy or buff is, of course, duller and the mealing will cover the cinnamon colour on breast and neck, but the same remarks apply here as to the yellow. When breeding these birds, it must be remembered that Cinnamon blood can only be introduced by the cock. If a cock canary of another breed is paired to a Cinnamon hen, they can only produce self, foul and variegated greens, cocks and hens without pink eyes. A Cinnamon cock paired to a normal dark-eyed hen can produce Cinnamons, cinnamon-marked, greens or green-marked birds; sex-linkage comes in here, and all the Cinnamons or cinnamon-marked birds will be hens. The green or green-marked birds from this cross are Cinnamon carriers and can produce cinnamon-marked birds and green-marked specimens when paired to black-eyed normal birds. When breeding Cinnamons, it may become necessary after a while to improve colour and perhaps virility; if so, a rich yellow self-green hen should be obtained and paired to the best yellow Cinnamon cock in your room. I know that the rule of yellow to buff is being broken in this instance, but it should be justified by results. All the self-greens bred from this cross should be kept, and the following year can be paired to other Cinnamons.

The Cinnamon Canary Club's Official Standard is as follows:

	Points
Colour	35
Shape and Type	20
Quality of Feather	15
Wing-carriage and Tail	10
Size	10
Condition, cleanliness, etc.	10
	100

THE YORKSHIRE CANARY
Plates 6–10

I have a very soft spot for the Yorkshires, for I started out with this breed of canary and in fact I have not been without them for half a century. It is known as 'the Gentleman of the Fancy', a very apt name for this large, slim, elegant bird with its swagger and verve. In early days it was said that the ideal bird should be able to pass through a wedding ring, though today it is doubtful whether an exhibition bird could pass through a small curtain ring. I feel that the present-day Yorkshire has progressed and is a better bird than ever before; in fact it has changed more than any other variety of canary, and since I started to breed them there have been no fewer than three major alterations. The bird should now be like an inverted carrot in shape.

There seems to be some doubt about its origin, and little had been heard about it until just over 100 years ago. The original Yorkshire canary was crossed with the Lancashire and the Belgian, which is how the length and position were obtained. (It is strange how a throwback can occur in pedigree breeding, for about 1930 I bred three yellow Yorkshire cocks in one nest; two were very good and won well for me, while the other was a typical Belgian that could have done equally well.) At the beginning of this century it was the most popular breed, following the formation of the Yorkshire Canary Club in 1894 and the drawing-up of an Official Standard.

The Yorkshire is a bird of position. It must stand on its top perch in the show cage 'like a guardsman', as the old-time fanciers put it.

When showing it should have swagger and verve, and grip the perch in an upright and fearless position. The slightest crouching is a bad fault. The Yorkshire must have 'legs', as without a length of leg it is nothing; one does see some birds with long, bare thighs, but even this is preferable to the short leg that seems to end at the knee joint. Any 'swimming' over the perch must also be avoided. As can be imagined this bird requires a great deal of training, and I advise all Yorkshire fanciers to make themselves a miniature show bench which can be collapsible and portable. All you need is a plank of wood about 6 feet long and two trestles or legs on a hinge to hold it. After the usual 'show cage on stock cage' training, the birds should be placed on this 'show bench', and it is a good plan to put one or two of the older ones in between to help train the youngsters. Handle the birds in the show cages as much as possible—this all helps in the training and induces the bird to 'show' to advantage. Always hold the cage from underneath, with your hand well below the bottom wire, and never hold it from the metal hoop at its top; the latter was originally fitted to hang the cage up in a shed, never for using when a bird was actually inside. Invite your friends, relatives and other fanciers to your birdroom, and then 'run out' the birds into the show cages for their inspection; this makes excellent training—you cannot run your bird in and out of the show cage too often.

A training stick is most useful; this should be about 16 inches long and made of wood about the size of a lead pencil. It should have a blunt end—when the birds are young this can be used to guide them into the show cage, and when they are trained it is usually sufficient to show it to them, whereupon they will take the hint and pop straight into the cage. (I remember in the old days the late Louis Dykes, in my opinion the greatest of all the Yorkshire fanciers, used to have just inside his birdroom an assortment of hats that he put on when working around the room; one was a top hat and another a lady's hat with a huge ostrich feather on it. These types of headgear were worn by the visitors to the shows in those days, so Louis made sure that his birds were not going to be startled by seeing a strange object on someone's head. He also placed his young birds in show cages, then into a show cage case, and took them upstairs. When he bounced the cage on the stairs, he reckoned that this was nothing compared with what the birds would have to put up with while on the railway, and he wanted them to get quite accustomed to being bumped about. His Yorkshires were seldom beaten, but when they were it was certainly not for lack of training.)

Two of the worst faults with a Yorkshire are open feathers on the breast and a 'hinged' tail, both throwbacks to the Lancashire and Belgian types. Should either appear in your stud you must be ruthless and eliminate the victims. The frilled breast was quite common 20 years ago, but I have not seen much of it in later years; the 'hinged' tail, however, is still all too prevalent. Breeding yellow to buff is essential here, as it is important to have a good-quality short feather; also the bird must maintain its size. A smallish yellow hen can usually get by, but even here a larger one may beat it; a good big one will always beat a good small one, all other things being equal, and there is no doubt that there are a lot of 'good big ones' in the Yorkshire fancy today.

Wing carriage is important; the wings should lie down the centre of the back and the tips just touch; to have crossed wings (known as 'scissoring') is a bad fault which is accentuated by a bad carriage in the bird. A good judge will jerk the show cage up and down a few times to give the bird a chance to lay its wings properly. Many writers and fanciers advocate 'tailing' the young birds. This is carried out after the first moult in order to obtain a little more length; the tail feathers are pulled out one by one, so that a new tail will grow which is just a little longer than the original. I myself never do this; I do not consider it justified, and in any case it will not improve any other feature of the bird. Recently I sent five young Yorkshires to five different Open Shows, and took best Yorkshire at each, yet not one of my birds was 'tailed'.

The Yorkshire is a reasonably free breeder and requires colour feeding. The show cage, which must be painted black all over, is made of wire fixed to a wooden base $3\frac{1}{8}$ inches deep. There is a trough at one side of the cage for seed, and at the opposite side there is a hole enabling the drinker to be attached from the outside; there is a perch for the seed and the drinker, and an additional perch above from which the bird must show itself. Perches must be oval with the bevelled edges uppermost. A plain zinc or plastic drinker is optional. Plain canary seed is the floor covering, and must also be used in the seed trough. (At one time, the use of any other kind of seed could have caused disqualification at a Patronage show; and this did in fact happen at a big show at Bradford where a well-known southern fancier had his birds disqualified through placing a little mixed seed in the cages. This rule has since been rescinded.) Yorkshires can be purchased from £10 to £15 a pair. Outstanding show birds will fetch as much as £100, and a pair of good birds that could win may bring up to £30 a pair. The same remarks already made in regard to the Norwich apply here. It was the Yorkshire that made me a champion canary exhibitor, for when I needed to obtain better birds I visited the next great Crystal Palace show where all the birds exhibited had to be for sale. I claimed a buff cock fourth in a class of 54, and a yellow hen third in a class of 46; both birds were exhibited and bred by the late D. Dawson (father of the leading Yorkshire fancier of today, Mr D. W. Dawson). The catalogue price was 27s. for the cock and 25s. for the hen, both prices including the show cage—those were the days!

The following is the Standard set down by the Yorkshire Canary Club:

		Points
Head	Full, round and cleanly defined. Backskull deep and carried back in line with rise of shoulders. Eye as near centre of head as possible. Shoulders proportionately broad, rounded and carried well up to and gradually merging into the head. Breast full and deep, corresponding to width and rise of shoulders and carried up full to base of beak which should be neat and fine.	20
Body	Well rounded and gradually tapering throughout to tail.	10
Position	Attitude erect with fearless carriage, legs long without being stilty, and slight lift behind.	25
Feather	Close, short and tight. Wings proportionately long and evenly carried down the centre of the back and firmly set on a compact and closely folded tail.	25
Size	Length approximately $6\frac{3}{4}$ inches with correspondingly symmetrical proportions.	10
Condition	Health, cleanliness and sound feathers, colour pure and level.	10
		100

There are quite a number of good white Yorkshires about, and special classes for them are provided at the Patronage shows. At one time there was a different breed of 'Yorkies' known as the 'Liverpool Greens'; they joined up with the Yorkshire Fancy and separate classes are now provided for them. The real greens are beautiful birds, a rich green with dark markings; they are not colour-fed, which shows up their rich natural green colour. Many so-called greens have a bronzy look, caused by too much cinnamon blood, but this is not the desired colour.

THE BORDER FANCY
Plates 11–17

The Border is the most popular of all the canaries. Originally known as the Cumberland Fancy, it originated in the Border counties of England and Scotland although little was heard about it until the 1880s. It soon became known as the 'Wee Gem', which indeed it was in those days compared with the other type canaries. In my opinion this name was unfortunate, because over the years nearly all types of canaries have developed and the modern Border cannot be described as 'wee' when we have the Lizard, the Gloster and the Fife. Indeed, the latter breed was produced in Scotland mainly because of the modern size of the Border. In addition to the older specialist societies, another has been formed called the Harry Norman Border Canary Society. Their standard of excellence is more or less the same as that of the other Border societies, except that their judges have to keep to the standard of $5\frac{1}{2}$ inches for the overall length of the bird and are, indeed, given a special measuring device to see that they do so.

After the First World War a number of large coarse-feathered birds were being shown as Borders, and I am sorry to say that many specialist judges who should have known better accepted these birds and gave them red tickets. There was soon an outcry, however; a number of Border judges simply refused to consider such birds and they gradually disappeared. I think the present-day Border is a really delightful bird; it is a free breeder and equally suitable for the novice and the champion, as competition is so keen in the champion classes that only a good bird has a chance of winning.

The Border should travel its perches with a jaunty action, and it is essential that there should be plenty of daylight apparent between the legs and the body; any birds that 'hug' the perches should be discarded. The Border should present a 'round' appearance from whatever angle it is viewed, and must have good-quality feathers; in other words, if it has not got first-class type and quality it is no good as a show bird. I have very little time myself for a Border much over $5\frac{1}{2}$ inches in length, for I remember the past and feel that larger birds should be discouraged. They should not be colour-fed; indeed a good natural-coloured yellow Border would—in my opinion—not be improved by colour-feeding. Being a bird of action it is imperative that it be well-trained. After the show cage has been used for a few days as previously described, gently lift it up with the bird inside, look at it for a few moments, then carefully replace the cage on the stock cage. Following a few more days of this treatment, hold the cage with one hand and bring the other hand up to the end where the bird is perching, causing it to fly to the opposite perch; then change the action so that it returns to its original perch. In this way you will soon get the bird flying from perch to perch, as will be required by the judge. I must emphasise that all movements when training birds, and all movements in the birdroom itself, should be slow and deliberate; sudden movement disturbs a bird, and a child suddenly pointing at it can cause more upset than the fancier moving around the room all day.

The Official Standard of the Border Fancy Canary Club is as follows:

		Points
Head	Small, round and neat-looking; beak, fine; eyes, central to roundness of head and body.	10
Body	Back well filled and nicely rounded, running in almost a straight line from a gentle rise over the shoulders to the point of the tail. Chest also nicely rounded, but neither heavy nor prominent, the line gradually tapering to the vent.	15
Wings	Compact and carried close to the body, just meeting at tips, at a little lower than the root of the tail.	10
Legs	Of medium length, showing little thigh, fine and in harmony with the other points, yet corresponding.	5
Plumage	Close, firm, fine in quality, presenting a smooth, glossy, silken appearance, free from frill or roughness.	10
Tail	Close-packed and narrow, being nicely rounded and filled in at the root.	5
Position	Semi-erect, standing at an angle of 60 degrees.	15
Carriage	Gay, jaunty, with full poise of head.	
Colour	Rich, soft and pure, as level in tint as possible throughout, but extreme depth and hardness such as colour-feeding gives are debarred.	15
Health	Condition and cleanliness shall have due weight.	10
Size	Not to exceed 5½ inches in length.	5
		100

The standard show cage for the Border is the Dewar pattern. I mention this because there are some very strict regulations regarding the show cage, and a novice buying some of the old-type cages in order to renovate them could find them a source of trouble. Oak husks only are allowed in the cage bottom, and the class labels must be stuck directly under the perch opposite the drinker. The perches must be $\frac{5}{8}$ inch in diameter, and are spirally turned with 16 teeth. I have known birds to be disqualified because these spirals were not correct. Coloured knobs to the seed drawer are prohibited, and so are round drinker holes in the show cage. The seed trough must have a slot, not holes.

There are more of the normal colours found in the Borders than in any of the other types of canary, and quite large classes of white ground are common. Classes are also provided for three-parts dark birds; these have to carry at least 75 per cent dark feathers, and if less they must be entered in the variegated classes. A 'ticked' bird is one that carries a single mark on head or body which can be covered with a sixpence, or three dark feathers on wing or tail side by side. A 'foul' bird is the opposite to the 'ticked' bird, that is to say, a dark bird with a single light mark.

THE GLOSTER FANCY
Plates 18–21

The Gloster is one of the more recent breeds. My old friend Mr A. W. Smith, one of the greatest canary fanciers who has ever lived, saw two entries in the novice Crested Canary class at the 1925 Crystal Palace Show where he was show manager. He realised the potential of these miniature Crests, and in deference to Mrs Rogerson of Cheltenham who had bred them, called the breed the Gloster Fancy. Through his efforts and encouragement, aided by that of other dedicated fanciers, he lived to see this delightful little canary take pride of place over all other breeds except the Border. As with the old Crests, there are really two types of Gloster, the crested bird known as the 'corona' and the plainhead known as the 'consort'. The aim of the original breeders of this bird was 'towards the diminutive' and this is still maintained—a good Gloster should not exceed $4\frac{3}{4}$ inches in length. Corona to consort should always be the mating, it does not matter which way. Yellow to buff should also be the rule, but unfortunately this may not be possible as there are very few yellows about, due to the partiality of past breeders for breeding buff to buff. (Judges were giving too much preference to the bigger crests bred this way against the smaller but better feathered yellows.) The Gloster Fancy is now encouraging the yellows, and I think this is only just in time, for if the trend of buff to buff had not been halted there would have been no yellows, and sooner or later 'lumps' would have appeared in force; in fact I have seen a few Glosters with these already. Ladies seem very partial to Glosters; they are small, neat, pleasing to the eye and above all are very fine breeders. Their cost is low, and even show birds can be purchased for as little as £3. The crest should radiate evenly all round the head from a definite centre, but this centre should not show a bare spot of skin; the feathers should lie neatly without any break in the circle, they should not show 'square' behind or be raised to look like horns. The consort should be of good feather, neat and above all have a good rounded head; the latter is important, for if any of its progeny should be coronas a good head will be essential to carry the right crest. Over the years I have judged many consorts with very mean heads indeed, so breeders should watch this point. Although the ideal Gloster should not be more than $4\frac{3}{4}$ inches in length, nevertheless

I would not be averse to breeding with a slightly larger bird, if it had all the necessary qualities. Birds always tend to breed down, which is why breeders of the large varieties are always struggling to maintain size. Smallness in itself is not to be aimed for; I have seen some very small, mean, racy types of birds that are not required. The cobby type should be the ideal.

Glosters are shown in a box-type show cage, which is black externally and eau-de-nil inside; the drinker must be black. They do not require colour-feeding, and taking everything into consideration are the ideal canary for the beginner. The Official Standard of the Gloster Fancy Canary Club is as follows:

		Points
Crest	Neatness. Regular, unbroken round shape, eye discernible.	15
	With definite 'centre'.	5
		20
or		
Consort	Head broad and round at every point, with good rise over centre of skull.	15
	Eyebrow heavy, showing brow.	5
		20
Body	Back well filled and wings laying closely thereto; full neck; chest nicely rounded without prominence.	20
Tail	Closely folded and well carried.	5
Plumage	Close, firm, giving a clear-cut appearance of natural colour.	15
Carriage	Alert, with quick lively movements.	10
Legs and feet	Medium length, without blemish.	5
Size	For tendency to the diminutive.	15
Condition	Health, cleanliness.	10
		100

THE NEW-COLOUR CANARIES
Plates 22–7

The New-Colour Canaries have emerged as the main development in the Fancy this century. Colour in birds (as against type) is quite a new idea originating from Mendel's *Principles of Heredity* and from the German Dr H. Dunker who published his book on genetics in 1929. The latter's theory was that it should be possible to produce a red canary by introducing a red factor into the genetic structure. This was made a little easier for would-be experimental breeders in that bird breeders in South America had already produced a hybrid that had proved fertile from the mating of a Hooded Siskin (*Spinus caculatus*, see plate 23) and a canary. In 1928 the late A. K. Gill bred the first Red Factor canaries in Britain from birds received from Dr Dunker. These birds were not truly red and the Doctor, who believed that the Hooded Siskin did not carry a yellow factor, decided to by-pass the normal canary with its yellow factor and to introduce the Dominant White canary in order to lose the yellow. (My own theory is that the Hooded Siskin does carry a yellow factor; I have seen a number of juvenile birds and all have carried a certain amount of yellow in their plumage. In any case, colour breeders today know that the yellow factor from the canary does not prevent production of the desired red colour.)

Just before the First World War and up to the early 1950s, the main classes for all the New Colours were Red Factors (plate 22). One of the strict rules of the Canary Colour Breeders' Association (a version, reformed in 1947, of the original Canary Colour Research Association which had been set up in 1938) was that no artificial colouring matter should be fed to the birds. It was quite evident, however, that at show after show these rules were being broken by a number of exhibitors. Winning birds were being sold and claimed at shows which, when the new owner moulted them out, had lost all their rich orange red and remained a wishy-washy colour. The Association then decided to bend the rules slightly and to allow the birds to be colour-fed—but only from things grown in the garden. Matters came more or less to a head in the early 1960s. I was judging an Open Show in Suffolk, and placed before me in both the champion and the novice classes were birds with bright-red plumage even on the flights and tails. I had no hesitation in disqualifying them as being artificially colour-fed. A few weeks later at an Open Show in East

Anglia, where some large classes of New Colours were being shown, a number of these highly coloured birds were once again placed before me to judge, and received the same treatment from me as at the previous show. My action caused a furore, as this was a Canary Colour Breeders' Patronage Show and, although it turned out that these birds had been bred by the same exhibitors in each case, some very caustic remarks were made as to my ability to judge, and some pungent letters appeared in *Cage and Aviary Birds* on the subject. I thought things had gone far enough and so, to settle the matter once and for all, I issued a challenge in the paper to the champion exhibitor concerned to allow one of the birds to be moulted out under instruction by a well-known canary breeder. I proposed that if the bird moulted out to anything like the original colour, I would donate £20 to the funds of the Canary Colour Breeders' Association. This challenge was refused.

Some time after these events the facts about Carophyll became common knowledge. It was first developed in Switzerland and used commercially for feeding to poultry in order to produce egg yolks of a good colour. As in the case of the Norwich canary nearly 100 years before, the Canary Colour Breeders' Association had now little option but to allow colour-feeding. There is no doubt that this decision, contrary as it was to all the Association stood for, was a courageous one. It has, of course, taken most of the competition out of the Red Factor classes; one now sees classes of, say, 10 birds all of which look exactly alike, though one or two may perhaps carry a greenish-bronzy colour showing that too much Carophyll Red has been fed. (This of course does help the judge to peg back a few, for it must be remembered that these birds are judged solely for colour.)

I should like to make it quite clear that since this brave decision the C.C.B.A. has gone from strength to strength. There are no fewer than 36 recognised colours at the time of writing, and no doubt by the time this book is published there will be more. The C.C.B.A.'s membership is well over 1,000. It will be appreciated that the standards of excellence for so many birds are too lengthy to be given here. The show cage is of the box type, black outside, with a black wire front; the interior is painted with Valspar powder blue, the seedhopper is at the bottom right-hand side of the cage, drinkers must be black and the floor covering should be mixed seed only. The popularity of these birds is far greater on the Continent, where in fact they greatly outnumber the type birds, but this is not yet the case in Britain. The following list should help to clear up some of the misunderstandings about the Continental and British names for the various colours:

THE CORRECT NAMES FOR THE NEW COLOURS

English	*Continental*
1. Melanin Pastel R/O	Pastel R/O Isabel
2. Melanin Pastel Blue	Pastel Blue
3. Opal Cinn R/O Dilute	Opal R/O Isabel
4. Opal Slate Blue	Opal Slate
5. Opal Dilute Green	Opal Agate
6. Opal Dilute Blue	Opal Silver Agate
7. Fawn	Silver Brown
8. Dimorphic Melanin Bronze	Mosaic Pastel Brown
9. Green	Green
10. Dilute Green	Agate
11. Cinnamon	Brown
12. Gold Cinn Dilute	Gold Isabel
13. Cinnamon R/O Dilute	R/O Isabel
14. Dilute Bronze	Bronze Agate
15. Red Orange Cinnamon	Red Brown
16. Bronze	Bronze
17. Rose Pastel	Ivory Rose
18. Rubino Cinnamon	Rubino Red Brown
19. Greywing Melanin Pastel Bronze	Greywing Pastel Bronze
20. Melanin Pastel Dilute Fawn	Pastel Silver Isabel
21. Dimorphic Bronze	Mosaic Bronze
22. Melanin Pastel Dilute Blue	Pastel Silver Agate
23. Rubino Cinn Dilute	Rubino Isabel
24. Rose Pastel Bronze	Ivory Bronze
25. Phaeo Dilute Cinn Albino	Phaeo Albino Isabel
26. Phaeo Cinnamon Albino	Phaeo Albino Brown
27. Phaeo Dilute Cinn Lutino	Phaeo Lutino Isabel
28. Phaeo Cinnamon Lutino	Phaeo Lutino Brown
29. Dimorphic Opal Bronze	Mosaic Opal Bronze
30. Dimorphic Melanin Pastel Bronze Opal	Mosaic Pastel Opal Bronze
31. Ivory Pastel	Ivory
32. Dimorphic Melanin R/O Cinn	Mosaic Pastel R/O Isabel
33. Rose Pastel Bronze Dilute	Ivory Bronze Agate
34. Opal Rose Pastel Bronze Dilute	Opal Ivory Bronze Agate
35. Melanin Pastel Cinn Dilute Gold	Pastel Gold Isabel
36. Melanin Pastel Cinn Dilute Gold	Pastel Silver Isabel

THE LIZARD CANARY
Plates 28–31

This unique canary is the only one bred for the pattern of its plumage, which as its name indicates should resemble the scales of a reptile. Our oldest breed of canary, its origin is unknown, though there is little doubt that it is a distinct mutation. In the old days it did not have a large following. This was probably because it was known as a one-year exhibition bird, and had to have a clear cap for exhibition purposes; this eliminated the majority of birds bred each year and also meant that breeding aimed at a clear cap tended to enlarge this so that it extended to the neck or face, thus becoming a serious fault. After the Second World War it was estimated that no more than 30 pairs of these birds were in existence. In May 1945, the late Robert H. Yates, together with Mr A. W. Smith, rallied around them all the known breeders and formed the Lizard Canary Association of Great Britain. One of these stalwarts, who in my opinion did more for the Lizard Fancy than any other man during the last 20 years or so, was the late Mr Fred Snelling, who kindly assisted in supplying the reference

clear-cap

non-cap

broken-cap

short-cap

over-cap

baldface

variations in broken-caps

THE VARYING CAPS OF THE LIZARD

for the drawing of the various 'caps'. In order to ensure the continued existence of the Lizards, the members of the Association agreed that they would only dispose of their surplus birds to fellow-members, and machinery was set up for this purpose. Luckily the birds proved to be very free breeders, and it was not long before the Association drew up classes for clear caps, broken caps and selfs; in addition, classes were provided for over-year birds. This put a different outlook on the whole question of exhibiting Lizards; many flocked to the Association, and well-filled classes are now common at the larger shows, over 100 being benched at leading shows.

I find the Lizard a very attractive bird, a free breeder and a good 'doer'. Among its other assets is the fact that there is no trouble in selling surplus birds, for the demand still exceeds the supply. Their price is moderate—£8 will buy a fair pair, and a good show bird can be purchased for as little as £6 or £7. A novice can buy a pair of birds from any champion, and possibly have 'best canary' at the Club Show with one of their young; this is because there is very little difference between a novice and a champion bird. It must be borne in mind that all the birds are descended from those few original pairs in 1945. 'Yorkies', Norwich and even Borders come in all kinds of shapes and sizes, but not the Lizard. There is little doubt that this is the canary for the beginner or novice to take up.

The yellow Lizard is known as a gold and the buff as a silver. The head is most important; it should have width of skull to emphasise the cap, which should cover the crown of the head, be of even size, oval and extend from the beak to the base of the skull. 'Spangling' is the name given to the main feature of the Lizard; this should be uniform and even, like rows of chains, gradually increasing in size and density, with no sign of greyness in colour. Wings must be dark with no suggestion of light feathering. The flanks should show well-defined markings which can be described as a row of stripes. The tail must be dark like the wings; the legs, feet and beak should also be dark. Special care must be taken with these birds, as any fighting and consequent loss of feathers could ruin them for show purposes, and it is likely that the new feathers would carry lighter markings. Any outstanding show birds should be caged separately until the end of the show season. The following is a glossary of terms used in connection with the Lizard:

Cloudy. Spangling that is not clearly defined.
Eyelash. A line of dark feathers over the eye, which improves the finish to the cap.

Grizzled. A greyish tint in the plumage.

Lacing. The edging of colour on the wing butts and coverts.

Lineage. Straight rows of spanglings.

Mooning. Another term for spangling.

Muddy Spangle. Like 'cloudy'; not clearly defined.

Rowing. Markings of breast and flanks. These must be clear and distinct and in lines.

Star Shoulder. The presence of a white feather or feathers in the wing-butts.

Work. The profusion of markings.

The Official Standard laid down by the Lizard Society is as follows:

		Points
Spangles	For regularity and distribution	25
Feather quality	For tightness and silkiness	15
Ground colour	For depth and evenness	10
Breast	For extent and regularity of rowings	10
Wings and tail		10
Cap	For neatness and shape	10
Covert feathers	For lacings	5
Eyelash	For regularity and clarity	5
Beak, legs and feet	For darkness	5
Steadiness and staging		5
		100

A bird on which the light area of feather constituting the cap encroaches on to the face, both below the eye and on the face, is termed a Baldface. This defect is usually caused by the continuous pairing of clear-cap to clear-cap. The correct pairing should be clear-cap to broken- or non-cap; the latter bird can be a great asset in the stud. Some fanciers pair two broken-cap birds, and still produce a fair percentage of clear-caps, but in my opinion it is best to carry out the correct pairing. Sometimes a bird will be bred that is over-capped; this means that instead of finishing at the base of the skull, the cap runs down into the nape of the neck. Though useless as an exhibition bird, an over-capped Lizard can be used in the breeding room if paired to a short- or non-capped bird.

THE ROLLER CANARY

This bird is cultivated for its song. Originally known as the German Canary, it came from the Hartz Mountains where it is estimated that about 400 families were engaged in the breeding and training of Rollers. Before the war the Hartz Mountain Roller, as it was then called, was very popular as a pet bird and many thousands were purchased.

The show or contest bird has to be carefully trained, and on no account should it hear the song of any other type of canary. This is a pity, as it precludes its participation in our National Shows; in the early days a large separate room was in fact provided for the Rollers, but these facilities are not now available and so the Fancy has drifted apart. The song is the sole basis for judging, no external markings or shape are taken into consideration. This is one branch of the Fancy where a faulty bird, i.e. one with a poor song, must be eliminated, for like a bad apple in a barrel it could spoil the whole stud.

The old method of training was to shut the bird in its small cage and to allow it to hear a prize singing bird known as a 'schoolmaster', but nowadays many breeders use a gramophone record or a tape recorder for this purpose. The British Standard recognises thirteen 'tours', i.e. well-defined short song passages, but very few birds are capable of singing them all. These 'tours' vary in contest value, and marks are given for the degree of perfection with which they are sung. They are delivered in a continuous rolling manner—hence the bird's name—and should all be soft and melodious. Many of the tours still retain their German names, such as Glucke, Glucke Roll, Schockel, and for a faulty tour Hard Aufzug.

Rollers are shown in a small wooden cage, fitted with a pair of shutters in front, and are trained to start singing directly these shutters arc opened. The song of the Roller is developed by careful feeding, which requires 50 per cent of the finest red rape seed mixed with plain canary; a little conditioning seed should be given two or three times a week. Without this red rape the song would not develop as required. Rollers are not the birds for those who are unable to devote a great deal of time to the hobby, as concentrated attention and training is essential. Of course, condition is everything, otherwise the birds would not sing. It must be realised that, although the hen has no contest value, for breeding purposes she can be as valuable as the cock; a pedigree hen, as in the type canaries, is essential. For all contests it is a rule that the birds must be close-ringed.

The scale of points agreed by the British Roller Canary Club and the National Roller Canary Society is as follows:

	Points
Hollow Roll	10
Bass	10
Water Glucke	10
Glucke	10
Glucke Roll	10
Hollow Bell	8
Schockel	8
Flutes	6
Water Roll	6
D.B.W.T.	5
Bell Roll	3
Bell Tour	2
General Effect	10
	—
	98
	—

(It will be noted that these points do not total 100 as in the type birds.)

The judges, who have to be very experienced, have the power to deduct 6 points for faulty Gluckes, 6 points for faulty Flutes, 3 points for Hard Aufzug and 6 points each for faulty Bells, Bad Nasal Tour and Ugly Interjections.

THE IRISH ROLLER

These must not be confused in any way with the Singing Roller canary, or for that matter with any other kind of canary whether type, pattern or colour. There is little doubt that this is the most popular canary in the Irish Republic, and my first introduction to the variety occurred when I was engaged to judge all the birds except the Rollers at an Open Show. I met my fellow-judge, Mrs Claffey, in Dublin, and as we travelled to the show I remarked that it would seem that I had most of the judging to do. 'Don't you believe it,' she replied. 'I bet the Rollers will outnumber all the other birds at the show.' They did, and she had more than 70 birds in some of her classes. There was no scale of points nor marks for excellence in regard to the birds, which came in all shapes and sizes and in all kinds of 'show' cages, some of which were simply wooden boxes with a wire front. After the judging the fun started. No one asked me anything, but they all milled round Mrs Claffey—Why did the little bird not win? It had won Ballymoney, Tipperary, etc., but not here. It was quite an education to hear Mrs Claffey giving all the reasons why the 'little birds' had not won, and I had difficulty in restraining my laughter. I later found out that Mrs Claffey had been engaged because fighting had broken out the year before, and they thought a woman would be better able to keep the peace!

Since those days I have judged Roller classes myself in various parts of Ireland. I pick the neatest, best-marked and finest-coloured bird that I can find, and so far have eluded trouble. A standard of points for these birds has recently been set up and the 'Irish Fancy' formed, but at the time of writing the old Roller is still much more popular in the provinces and country districts and I doubt if the standard of points will ever be universally followed. After all, being of Irish extraction myself, I can see the attraction in showing this variety—you can have endless arguments about the judging and no one can say you are wrong, not even the judge!

THE CRESTED CANARY
Plates 34–5

This is one of our oldest canaries and records of it go back to about the 1750s. It was first known as the 'Turncrown', and early in this century as the 'King of the Fancy'. During the nineteenth century it was at the height of its popularity, and large classes were usual at most of the leading shows; towards the end of the century it became such a craze that really large amounts of money were paid for good Crests, sometimes as much as £50 for a single bird. The climax came when a man paid £265 to one breeder for three birds. This was a tremendous sum in those days, for one could buy a working-class house for about £60 at that time. It was then considered that the Crests were only for rich men, and from that time onwards their popularity steadily declined. Furthermore, the old practice of double buffing had become rampant in an effort to produce still larger crests, and of course the result was 'lumps'.

I have watched the progress of these birds carefully in recent years, but I am sorry to say that they are hardly holding their own, despite the mighty efforts of stalwarts like L. Franz, who is really doing everything possible to keep this variety going. The breed received a very good advertisement when a Crested Canary was made Supreme Champion bird at the National Show in 1960, but the potentialities of this great win were not properly realised, owing probably to a great lack of stock. It is essential, if this breed is to survive, that a number of novices take it up. In my early days, some of the judges I knew used to carry around a 4s. piece for measuring the crest. It should radiate from the centre of the head and extend over the beak to the back of the head about level with the eyes, the latter being almost hidden. The crest must be shapely, large and dense, the feathers of a broad and leafy texture. The Crested Canary is a large bird and should possess a very large head, a short, thick neck and a broad, deep body—not unlike the requirements for a Norwich; but here the resemblance ends, for the Crest carries a profusion of feathers which would not be tolerated in the Norwich. As with all crested canaries, it is necessary to mate two types in order to produce a good crest; the plain-headed variety is known as the Crest-bred, and the other as the Crest. When pairing, it does not matter which sex is the Crest or the Crest-bred. Buff should be paired to yellow, but as with the Gloster this is not always easy as there are more buffs than yellows in existence. Long feathers have to be bred all over the bird in order to obtain sufficient length to form a good crest, and this causes some of the best specimens to look a bit feathery. But this is not regarded as a fault, for it is the crest that is all-important provided the body is up to standard. Breeding these birds today is something of a challenge; compared with the more popular breeds they are not easy, but success will bring its own rewards. I for one would very much like to see this grand old breed grace our shows with full classes once again. There was a slight improvement with the entry at the last National, but only two entries in the novice classes.

THE FIFE FANCY
Plate 39

This is the latest addition to the ranks of the Exhibition Canary. The breed was brought about through the disappointment of a number of Border exhibitors as their 'Wee Gem' became larger and larger. At the National Shows in the late 1950s, the miniature class was very well supported, the majority of entries being Borders. In 1957 a meeting was called at Kirkcaldy in Scotland, and there the Fife Fancy Canary Club was formed. In two or three years this canary's popularity grew, and quite a number of clubs in Scotland and the north of England had good entries under the patronage of the F.F.C.C. Its popularity did not extend to the south, however, and despite the fact that special classes were put on at the National Show they were so poorly supported that the birds have been relegated to the Any Other Canary Class. Yet at the Scottish National Show over 100 birds have been entered at a time.

The Fife Fancy is in fact a miniature Border, and the scale of points is practically the same for both, the main point of difference being that no bird can be considered a Fife Fancy if it is over $4\frac{1}{2}$ inches long. A Border show cage is used for exhibiting this variety. They are very free breeders and would be a good variety for the beginner to canary breeding to start with. Stock is easy to obtain and £4 or £5 will buy a good pair.

THE FRILL
Plate 33

Unlike the Crested Canary the Frill is more than holding its own today, and thirty-six entries were seen at the last National Show. In the eighteenth century the Frill was known as the old Dutch Canary, but since then several varieties have spread to different countries. There are now the Dutch, Italian and Parisian varieties, and the Japanese have produced a miniature edition and extended it to the red factor— I should imagine these are most attractive. The finest example of the Frilled Canary is the Parisian Frill.

Many Frills are quite large birds well over 8 inches in length. The three main kinds are called the Mantle (*le Manteau*), the Jabot and the Fins. The Mantle is so called because of the feathers, which are parted down the back and fall symmetrically. The Jabot is the name given to the chest feathers, which should be undulating and wavy and curl inwards; they should come from each side of the breast to form a ruffle, meeting in the middle like a closed shell called the Craw. The Fins are the long feathers, well frilled, that come from the thighs and sweep upwards around the wings. Some of the Continental exhibitors use a pair of miniature curling tongs to ensure that the feathers curl in the right direction.

A good Frill is a very attractive bird, a bad one is a monstrosity. These birds are fairly good breeders, and considering that there are not many about, their price is reasonable; a pair fetches from £15.

THE BELGIAN CANARY
Plate 38

This is another of the oldest breeds of canary, and is a bird of position and shape only. To be quite frank, it appears to be deformed, and I well remember my wife saying to me in the early days that if I introduced this monstrosity into my birdroom, she would no longer attend to the needs of my birds when I was away. Perhaps she was a bit harsh in her judgement, but nevertheless I cannot see the Belgian making a wide appeal to the present-day fancier. It is well known that this bird was never a reliable breeder, and as a general rule the eggs are placed under foster parents to act as feeders. Also, it takes a very great deal of time to train them up to show standard, time which the ordinary modern fancier would not consider giving.

The Belgian has been used extensively in the past for breeding other varieties of canary, and there is no doubt that it is one of the direct ancestors of the Yorkshire and the Scotch Fancy to name but two. It was in demand during the 1850s, and many changed hands at around the £20 mark, a small fortune for those days.

This bird has a very small snakey head, such as was very apparent in many Yorkshires in the old days but is rarely seen today. Feather and colour are not considered; as already stated, it is only shape and position that count—in fact, out of 100 points given for show only a maximum of 4 is given for feather. The neck can be elongated or shortened according to the stance the bird adopts. When it is not showing, the neck and head are at right-angles to the body, the head being level with the shoulders.

At the last National Show no less than 16 Belgians were on view, seven of which came from Belgium, the most seen for over fifty years.

THE SCOTCH FANCY
Plate 32

This canary is known as the 'Bird O'Circle', due to its formation of a semicircular shape from the head to the tip of the tail when in show position. This unusually shaped bird has always been found more extensively in Scotland and the north of England; it has never been very popular in the south, although I did see good classes down south when I was a lad before the First World War. Its greatest following was in Glasgow, where in fact it was called the 'Glasgow Don'. In the 1850s more than 1,000 birds were entered at some of the leading Scottish shows. I am sorry to say that its popularity in Scotland has now declined, and every year there seem to be fewer shown; the last fair classes that I saw were at the Scottish National in the early 1960s, when I had the pleasure of judging them. They were exhibited by one or two fanciers only, to whom great credit must go for keeping the breed going. I am pleased to see that the Scottish National still has a special section for these birds. There does seem to be a demand for the Scotch Fancy abroad, and it is just possible that there could be a revival. I sincerely hope that this will come about.

The Scotch Fancy should have a small head, a little rounder than the Belgian; the neck is slender and long, the shoulders well-filled yet narrow and rounded; wings should be long and carried close to the body; long well-braced legs are essential, and good feather is also important. In fact, this bird must be top quality in every way to be 100 per cent for show. It should have position, also posture and type and, like the Border, good action; it should be a free mover showing character and excellent carriage, and the movement from perch to perch—known as 'travelling'—should be perfectly carried out. This can only be achieved by extensive training, which the few birds I have seen latterly do not seem to have had; this situation would not have suited the judges in past years, when no fewer than 25 points out of 100 were allocated for this particular attribute. Since writing the above 25 birds were entered at the National in the two classes.

THE LANCASHIRE CANARY
Plates 36, 37

This was our largest canary, but it is now many years since I saw a true Lancashire. Two were shown at a National Show in the 1960s, but they were not the size of the old birds. Their decline was due to a number of factors: they were not free breeders, and those that were bred were in great demand for the development of other varieties. Also, mule breeders were always looking for Lancashire hens to give size to their mules, these being especially suitable for Linnet mules. I myself tried to purchase some hens between the wars, as did a number of my London friends, and of course any purchased by us for mule breeding were lost to the Lancashire Fancy.

As the name suggests its stronghold was in Lancashire, and at the end of the last century it had pride of place in the main shows in that county, outnumbering all the other varieties put together with the possible exception of the Lizard Canary which was also popular with Lancastrians. The Lancashire was a crested variety, and like all crested birds the 'Coppy' had the crest and the 'Plainhead' had none. The crest was, however, quite different, and instead of being more or less round as in all the other varieties it was a horseshoe shape, with the feathers radiating from the centre over the beak and eyes, while at the back of the head they lay flat and merged into the back of the neck. Although the Coppy takes pride of place, carriage and contour are very important; the body should be long and tapering with a full breast and broad straight back, wings and tail long and compact, and the legs strong and very straight, giving the bird a swaggering and bold appearance. When in a show cage there is a slight curve, but this is not considered a fault. There are four colour types for show purposes: clear yellow, clear buff, ticked yellow and ticked buff. Variegated birds were not catered for, but this ruling did not help the Fancy, and in the event of a revival of the breed I would expect to see classes for the variegated category. Thanks to the efforts of Mr G. T. Dodwell, the Chairman of the O.V.C.A., this variety is on the way back.

THE LONDON FANCY
Plate 40

There is no doubt that this breed has completely disappeared, and alone among all the canaries it seems to be irretrievable, since we have lost its black inheritance. The last time a supposed class of these birds was seen was at the Crystal Palace Show in 1931. After the judging Mr A. W. Smith, the show manager, lodged a protest concerning these birds and managed to remove the black markings from the birds. The owner was quite indignant, asking what he expected, that there never was a true London Fancy and they were always 'prepared'. This statement got around, and even today there are still a number of old-timers who really believe it to be true. Of course there were London Fancies. Mr H. Roberson told me that his father had a large stud, and he reckoned that they bred 90 per cent true. In 1910 he and his father decided not to continue breeding London Fancies as they had had their day, being a one-year-only show bird. In 1914 he went on active service, and after the war all that remained of the London Fancies were half a dozen aged specimens. He was interested in British birds at that time, so the Fancy just died out. Later he regained his interest in canaries and he and others tried to revive the breed, but they could not introduce the black inheritance and that was that.

It is a great pity that this bird has disappeared, because it was a very beautiful canary, its plumage being a rich golden yellow with black wings and tail markings in delightful contrast. It was one of our oldest canaries and, as already mentioned, the original birds had black spots. Most authorities believe that it was closely related to the Lizard, and consider that the original parentage of both types involved birds other than canaries, possibly a British Redpoll or a similar bird carrying a black inheritance. Both the London Fancy and the Lizard look like British finches when in nest feather, unlike every other type of canary. Some years ago I bred what looked like a perfect London Fancy in a nest of Norwich Canaries, but although the markings were very dark, they were not jet-black.

Since I wrote the above an association has been formed called the Old Varieties Canary Association. I have the honour to be President of this association which hopes to try and revive various old varieties.

CANARY HYBRIDS
Plates 41–8

Introduction

Canary hybrids were called 'mules' by the older generations of fanciers because, like the mammal mule, they cannot reproduce. Even today most fanciers use the word to differentiate between the British × canary and the British × British bird. The canary mule, as we will call it, has been bred for a very long time—mainly, I believe, because of the challenge it offers to the breeder, who is after all trying to defy Nature. Nearly every canary breeder has attempted 'muling' at one time or another—not always with success I am bound to say.

Canaries have now been bred with most of the British finches, even the crossbill, but pairings with the hawfinch and bramblefinch have yet to be achieved; nor so far has any of the buntings been crossed with success. A good mule is very valuable—a light mule can fetch up to £100. In fact, I knew of a clear siskin mule that changed hands for £200 in the early 1950s, and even a good dark mule will fetch £25 without much difficulty, so the rewards in this branch of the hobby are quite considerable. The National British Bird and Mule Club offer a gold medal to any of their members for a first cross, and such a bird usually sweeps all before it on the Show Bench. Even poor specimens are in demand, as they are excellent songsters.

The hens, I am sorry to say, have very little value indeed, since they do not sing and of course cannot breed; however, they will lay eggs and rear other birds, and so they can be of some value in the canary room. Many claim that they have had fertile mules; this is possible, but the chances are so remote that they can be ignored by the practical breeder. In mule breeding it must be remembered that as a general rule the canary will come into breeding condition before the finch. It is therefore best to use a wire slide to separate the pair from about February onwards after they have run together all the winter. The idea of separating them is that, in order to get the finch into breeding condition at the same time as the canary, extra foods including soaked seeds, egg food, condition seed and so on can be fed to it while the canary is kept on a plainer diet. Despite all this it is quite likely that the first clutch of eggs will be clear; one must just try again and again. The goldfinch, in particular, is very late in coming into breeding condition and it is sometimes well into June before it is really fit. Some canary breeders take a nest or even two from a canary hen paired to a cock canary, and then pair up very late for a third nest with a goldfinch. Neither a mule breeder nor a leading canary breeder would be interested in this method, since the demands on a hen are too heavy, but it is used with a fair amount of success. Mules are shown in the standard British seed-eater cages which would be used for the finch partner in the pairing. The cages are of the box type, painted green inside and black outside; the wire front is green and the outside of the drinker black.

Breeding

In the majority of cases the mule breeder will find it easier to breed with a male finch and a female canary. An exception to this is the female greenfinch, which is almost as reliable as the canary. Another exception is the bullfinch, since so far as is known the male bullfinch has never sired anything but a bullfinch. I do not know why this should be, but it is a fact, so here the rule must be canary × bullfinch. (It is the regular practice to place the male first in describing any kind of hybrid.) To breed exhibition mules the Norwich or a Norwich-type canary must be used; the actual breeding methods are much the same as those for breeding canaries.

As already stated, the finches do not usually come into breeding condition early in the year, but this can be dealt with as suggested earlier. The finch is less likely to be tame than the canary, and so it is a good plan to fix a piece of cardboard on the front of the cage, just to shield the nest pan from view. I use a small wooden box-type nest with a perforated zinc bottom for mule breeding. Since mule breeding is against nature, it is essential that both birds should be really super-fit. If they are not bursting with life and energy, you are doomed to failure. Plenty of soaked seed, dandelion leaves and roots should be given daily in early spring, and later when chickweed is available it should be fed by the handful. For rearing purposes ample quantities of soaked seed, egg food, chickweed plus a little bread and milk should be given.

For exhibition purposes these birds must be colour-fed, adopting the same procedure as already given for canaries. It sometimes happens that adult mules will not eat soft food. Should this happen to you, mix an egg-cup full of olive oil with a pound of seed, thoroughly mix in the red pepper and stir well for some minutes. Then leave for 48 hours, by which time the olive oil will have carried the colouring agent right into the seed. This will have the same effect, or better, than the usual method of colour-feeding.

One sure way to breed mules is to have an aviary outdoors. Place plenty of gorse, privet, pea-sticks, etc., in the corners of the aviary, and then turn in half a dozen canaries and two or three different male finches. Throw plenty of seeding chickweed, soaked seed and so on into the aviary, so that the birds become breeding fit in their own time; in this way you are almost certain to obtain some mules. There are two disadvantages to this: firstly, you cannot select the partners and you do not know what kind of mules you will breed; secondly, the nest is usually in the thickest part of the 'shrubbery', so you are unable to assist the young in any way if the hen stops feeding. Also, of course, you cannot try for the bullfinch cross, since if you put in a male canary it would mate naturally with the other canary hens and the result would be young canaries!

Aims for the mule breeder

There are three standards of perfection to aim for in all mules: the Clear, the Even-marked and the Self-Dark. The Clear looks just like a canary to the uninitiated, but the expert can recognise its parentage. The same applies to the Even-marked bird; its marks should be seen as the technical marks on the Yorkshire canary—two eye ticks are classed as a two-pointer, while a four-pointer would be evenly marked on both eyes and both wings and nowhere else. The Yorkshire canaries can have other marks besides the technical, but no other marks are allowed in the standard of perfection for Even-marked mules.

The third standard of perfection is the Self-Dark. To breed a Clear or a light mule, as a bird is designated when more than half of its feathers are light, you must use a finch that is carrying a light gene. Many mule breeders will disagree with me on this score, but I am confident that it is so. The late George Weston and I carried out a very comprehensive study of all the light mules we could find 25 years ago, and in every case discovered that the finch was responsible. A typical example occurred at a tent show being run by the Greenford C.B.S. in the local park. There was a nice class of dark mules on show, and a visitor came up to the show manager, Sid Hebert, and myself and said how he liked them. He had been breeding mules for some years but all his were most disappointing and they looked just like canaries! We looked at him in amazement and wondered if he was joking, but he proved to be right. There were Clears, marked and variegated (all from Roller canaries) and one goldfinch cock. We explained to him that if these birds were a little larger they would be worth a small fortune, and advised him to obtain some good yellow Norwich hens for the next breeding season, but he lost the goldfinch during the moult. He was not discouraged by this, but hoped to be able to get another and breed many light mules; however, he never bred a light feather from that day to this.

In the old days the mule breeders used to concentrate on the hen canary for the light mules and breed clear canary to clear, until all the markings and colour were eliminated. These were then known as Sib-bred hens, valuable no doubt if the cock finch carried a light gene but otherwise quite useless.

The Dark mule should be cobby and chubby; this is why the Norwich-type canary is so important. A yellow-green bird is invaluable for this cross, and if possible a highly variegated yellow should be used. The yellow or jonque mule is the one that all aim for; a big good buff or mealy greenfinch mule is acceptable, but a good yellow will always have the advantage. In the old days a buff goldfinch mule had no value at all as a show bird, but today special classes are put on for buffs at the larger shows, the reason being that they stand very little chance if classed with the good yellows. A small patch of light feathers or even a single light feather in flight or tail in a dark mule make it useless for exhibition, so it can be appreciated that it is best to use variegated or self hens when possible. I *have* bred good dark mules from clear yellow hens, but in such cases there is always the chance of a light feather or two turning up.

SCALE OF POINTS FOR EXHIBITION CANARY HYBRIDS

Clear, lightly ticked and lightly variegated
canary hybrids

		Points
Size	To be of good size, compatible with that of the parents.	10
Shape	To be of stout cone shape, with broad bold head, and close fitting wings and tail.	10
Markings	To be distinctly characteristic of both parents, and the clearer the plumage the better.	20
Colour	To be deep and rich in colour naturally, and when colour-fed to be considerably intensified.	10
Quality	The plumage to exhibit the highest possible smooth, glossy surface throughout.	20
Condition	To be sound in condition in every part.	15
Steadiness	The bolder and firmer the stand on the perch the better.	10
Staging	To be shown in clean condition and in a neat and clean cage.	5
		100

Faults	Wildness, crouching, puffiness, broken or missing feathers, deformities of body, wings, legs or feet, poor quality of markings, bad condition, etc.

		Points
Size	To be of good size, compatible with that of the parents.	10
Shape	To be of stout cone shape, with broad bold head, and close fitting wings and tail.	10
Markings	Whether eyes, wings or tail, any or all to be as even on both sides of the bird as possible, and not to run beyond the technical regions of markings proper.	35
Colour	To be rich and deep in tone naturally and when colour-fed to be very highly intensified.	10
Quality	The feathers to be perfect and like wax, with a satin-like surface.	10
Condition	To be of the very best in every respect.	10
Steadiness	The bolder and firmer the position on the perch the better.	10
Staging	To be shown in clean condition and in a neat and clean cage.	5
		100

Faults   Badly balanced markings; markings running beyond their proper regions, or being so faint and indistinct that they barely outline the character of the mark; crouching; poor shape; poor feather; deformity in any part; wildness; undersize. All these discount points when present.

Dark canary hybrids

The standard is the same as that of the Clear, except that a dark bird without any light feathers is required.

A note on the American finches

There is no reason at all why a number of the American finches should not hybridise with canaries. I have bred a purple finch × canary, a purple finch × British greenfinch and housefinch × greenfinch. I suggest the following might be bred and would make very attractive and excellent singing birds: gray-crowned rosy finch, pine siskin, song sparrow, chipping sparrow, slate-coloured junco, field sparrow and indeed any of the different finches called sparrows that are found in different parts of the United States. The crossbill has been crossed with a canary in England, and the result was a truly handsome bird that took best Hybrid at the National Show held at Olympia in London. It may be that a number of these suggested crosses have already been achieved, but we have no official knowledge of any in Britain so far. I have not suggested any of the bunting family, since we have bred no hybrids from this family as yet. Due to the strict laws governing the export of birds from the United States, the private British aviculturist cannot obtain any birds either for straight breeding or for hybridising. My own successes were achieved in the 1940s.

SPECIALIST SOCIETIES

Borders

Border Fancy Canary Club
British Border Fancy Canary Club
Eastern Counties Border Fancy Canary Club
Green Cinnamon and White Border Canary Club
International Border Breeders Association
Midland Counties Border Fancy Canary Club
Northern Ireland Border Fancy Canary Club
Southern Border Fancy Canary Club
Western Counties Border Fancy Canary Club

Norwich

East Anglian Norwich Plainhead Club
Midland Counties Norwich Plainhead Club
Norwich Plainhead Canary Club
Scottish Plainhead Club
Southern Norwich Plainhead Canary Club

Yorkshires

Eastern Yorkshire Canary Club
Lancashire Yorkshire Canary Club
Midland Yorkshire Canary Club
Southern Yorkshire Canary Club
Western Yorkshire Canary Club
Yorkshire Canary Club
Yorkshire Canary Club of Scotland

Glosters

Eire Gloster Club
Gloster Fancy Canary Club
Midland Gloster Fancy Association
Scottish Gloster Fancy Canary Club
Southern Gloster Fancy Canary Club
Western Gloster Fancy Canary Club

New Colours

Canary Colour Breeders Association
Scottish Canary Colour Breeders Association

Lizards

Lizard Canary Association of Great Britain

Fife Fancy

Fife Fancy Canary Club

Old Varieties

The Old Varieties Canary Association

The names and addresses of the Hon Secs. of the various Specialist Societies can be obtained from the Editor, *Cage & Aviary Birds*, 161/166 Fleet St., London E.C.4. This is a weekly publication of great interest to all bird keepers and all types of canaries are advertised for sale every week.

GLOSSARY

Broken-cap Refers to the mixing of light and dark feathers on top of the Lizard's head.

Buff and yellow Types of feather; the edges of buff feather are tipped with white which gives a frosted appearance absent in yellow.

Cap The clear patch of feathers, either yellow or buff, on the head of the Lizard.

Cages, show or stock Stock cage: where the bird is kept; show cage: that used for shows.

Cobby The ideal shape of the Norwich: body short and chubby.

Coppy The crest of feathers on the Lancashire's head.

Club Show A show run by a club purely for its own members.

Clear Describes a bird with no dark feathers.

Colour-feeding *See* pp. 37–40.

Corona and consort These refer to the Gloster: the corona carrying a crest and the consort having a plainhead.

Dilute A bird whose dark pigments are very pale due to the dilute gene.

Dominant character Occurs when, on breeding with two birds that show contrasting features, one dominant, one recessive, all the young show the characteristics of the dominant parent.

Double buffing Pairing two buff birds to obtain larger feathers; very seldom advisable.

Egg-binding *See* p. 33.

Even-marked Carrying the same marks or dark feathers on either side of the eyes or tail, or on the flights.

Flights The large quill feathers in the wings.

Flighted A bird that is over a year old and has gained its adult flight feathers.

Flue The down next to the skin.

Foul Refers to a dark bird with one light mark.

Frosted *See* Buff.

Genes Inheritable bodies which cause hereditary characteristics.

Ground colour General colour underlying distinctive markings, e.g. yellow or buff of the Lizard.

Heavily variegated Refers to a bird having more than one half of its body a dark colour.

Hinged tail Term used of a tail which droops instead of being aligned with the body.

Hot Refers to a deep rich orange colour due to colour-feeding.

In-bred Bred from parents related to each other.

Jonque An old term used for yellow, especially when the bird has been bred from two yellows.

Lacing Markings on the margins of the feathers on the wing butts, tail and flight feathers of the Lizard.

Lethal Describes a pairing which carries a factor that will cause the death of the young chick.

Lightly variegated The opposite to heavily variegated.

Line-bred *See* In-bred.

Mandible The horny part of a bird's beak.

Mealy *See* Buff.

Nape The back part of the neck nearest to the skull.

Nest feather The first plumage of a young bird when it leaves the nest.

Non-capped Term used when the thumbnail patch of light feathers on top of the Lizard's head is absent.

Non-fed A bird of natural colour, which has not been colour-fed.

National Show The annual show run by *Cage and Aviary Birds* magazine at Alexandra Palace.

Open Show A show run by a club or specialist society and open to all.

Orange ground Variation from yellow ground, brought about by the introduction of the Hooded Siskin.

Over-year *See* Flighted.

Outcross Refers to the introduction of a bird from another strain to improve some feature.

Pin feather A feather still in quill which has just come through the skin.

Pipe-tailed Describes a canary whose tail feathers are closely and tightly set.

Position The stance the bird takes in the show cage.

Plainhead A bird with no crest; a term used of Norwich and Lancashire canaries.

Recessive *See* Dominant character.

Red factor Orange canary, *see* Orange ground.

Round Describes a bird whose outline appears curved from any angle.

Rowing On the Lizard, the arrangement of the spots forming the spangling.

Self Term used for a cinnamon or green bird whose plumage is unbroken by any other colour.

Scissoring A term used to denote the crossing of the flights.

Soft moult *See* p. 22.

Spangling The lines of small black spots on the plumage of a Lizard.

Square The opposite to 'round' (*q.v.*).

Stormer A term used for an exceptional bird.

Tailing The practice of removing the first tail from a Yorkshire to obtain a little more length in the new tail.

Taper The tapering away of the body from the chest downwards.

Ticked Describes a clear bird carrying a dark mark that can be covered by a sixpence. In the Yorkshire this can be a very large patch of dark feathers.

Type The various points laid down by the specialist societies to distinguish each breed.

Unflighted *See* Flighted.

INDEX

Bold figures refer to the colour plates